THE
OTHER SIDE
OF WAR

by

Herbert M. Youngdahl

Robert D. Reed Publishers • San Francisco, California

Robert D. Reed Publishers
750 La Playa Street, Suite 647
San Francisco, CA 94121
Phone: 650-994-6570 • Fax: -6579
Email: 4bobreed@msn.com
Website: www.rdrpublishers.com

Typesetters: Marge Ann Wimpee
               and Pamela D. Jacobs, M.A.
Editors: Doretta Youngdahl
               and Pamela D. Jacobs, M.A.
Cover by: Julia A. Gaskill

ISBN 1-885003-57-9

Library of Congress Catalogue Number: 00-102832

Manufactured, Typeset, and Printed in the United States

To Doretta,
without her there
would be no book

NOTE TO THE READER

All of the stories in this book are based on true experiences, except one story is fiction. It was included to show the destructive capabilities of trench mortars. You cannot hide from mortars unless you're in an inaccessible place.

CONTENTS
Young Sarge Series

FOREWORD

Herbert Youngdahl remembers many incidents during his twenty-three years of military service. He started as a private and retired as a captain. He chased Germans from North Africa, through the Italian Campaign, to Germany. He served in Korea. He received the Bronze Star and many other medals.

Life is the luck of the draw. When you were born, what was your environment? What was your niche in life? Most importantly, what did you do with your circumstances?

These pages describe the way that it was. This is the way Herb remembers things to relate. He wrote everything down on paper to read and think about.

What lessons there are in this part of life is up to you to determine. Fate moves in mysterious ways. Many men lost their lives and many made it through. There were prisoners of war and those missing in action. No one can make it through battles without being scarred in some way. Herb had to find humor somewhere along the way because it was there.

Our country should be thankful that we have the Herbert Youngdahls, for our future as a country depends on it.

— Donald B. Nelson
Chaplain
VFW Post 10245

INTRODUCTION

I was born in the Midwest in Lake City, Iowa on September 2, 1921. I attended first grade in Central K-12 school. I loved elementary school and was fairly eager. I collected attendance slips and was a crossing guard.

My parents, Verner and Eva Youngdahl, moved our family to the big city — Sioux City, Iowa on the banks of the Missouri River — in search of their fortune. That's where I attended and graduated from Central High School.

Almost every week night I worked setting pins in a local bowling alley. It was closed on weekends so many weekends I was fortunate to find work in one of the big bowling alleys downtown. Sometimes I'd set over one hundred lines in one day. That was big money to take home — but exhausting work. Every dime I made went to my mother. She and my father had divorced.

Some Monday mornings my mother rolled me over, took a look at me, and told me to go back to sleep. She'd write a note to my school. Once I quit school but that was a big mistake. When my Irish mother got through with me I gladly returned to school.

I always paid for my lunch. Every noon I ate two large rolls and drank milk, which cost ten cents. (I actually never saw the school cafeteria until years later on a tour during a class reunion.)

Even though I was small, I joined the school's second football team. Unfortunately I had to drop out because of my exhausting work at the bowling alley.

Doretta (my future wife) and I began a friendship in junior high school. We were very poor but industrious. If we had two nickels, we would go to a picture show. With one nickel, I could buy a candy bar and share it with Doretta and her sister Mary.

Doretta and I went out on Sundays for wild times. For the dollar that my mother allotted us we could go to a dance. (Doretta sold tickets for her dad at the local Moose Hall and I would get in for free.) We gorged ourselves on hot dogs, drank Coke, enjoyed bowling, and had a hell of a good time just being together.

We married and eventually had three children. (Now we are blessed with six grandchildren and three great grandchildren.) I was not present when my children were born. I managed to get sent overseas until all was clear back home. My son was born while I was in Ireland. He was over two years old before I met him. There was (and still may be) a conflict when I came home and usurped his position in the household.

During the Korean Conflict I was appointed to the rank of Second Lieutenant. Almost all of us WWII combat sergeants were promoted. It seems they needed officers badly and we made exceptionally good officers.

I spent a total of twenty-three years in the Army. I was an enlisted man for fourteen years and an officer for eight years. My Unit, the 34th Iowa National Guard Division, set the record of over 500 days in combat in WWII. I was with them for most of those days. We had over a year's combat before the great invasion into Europe. When we heard about it, we remarked that we hoped the invasion would draw enemy troops from Italy and take some of the pressure off of us. Germans always held the high ground.

I fought in Africa and Italy. In Northern Italy the Company Commander called me in and informed me that I was no longer stable enough to command my platoon. At twenty-one years old, I was fired. It seems that I developed battle fatigue and no longer could be trusted with the lives of my soldiers. It was time for me to go to the rear. I left Europe and returned home to Sioux City.

Fortunately I made good use of the GI Bill. I bought two homes — one in San Antonio, Texas and one home (where Doretta and I live now) in the beautiful coastal town of Pacifica, California.

I attended San Francisco State University, where I earned a B.A. in Social Science, a Master's degree in Education of Exceptional Children, and Credentials in General Social Science, the Physically Handicapped, and Education of the Visually Impaired. I worked hard to keep my grade point average about 3.8 (out of 4.0). I always needed a lot of sleep so thanks to my coaches who monitored study hall I managed to catch up on sleep through all of my study periods. I would put my head down on the desk and sleep — perhaps even dream of writing a book some day.

For fifteen years I taught in the San Francisco Unified School District. Now I am retired and receive a modest pension.

Doretta and I enjoy participating in at least one service to our community every day. We are dedicated to people and will go to any length to help others. She is an officer in the American Legion Auxiliary. I am an officer in the American Legion and an active member of the Veterans of Foreign War (VFW). We run a Vision Support Group and are involved with many activities at our Community Center.

Writing this book has been a long-term dream that has finally become a reality. I have always had an active imagination and have enjoyed creative projects. My hope is that a successful book will help to support the organizations in which we are involved. I am constantly transporting various items for our local organizations and Veterans' Hospitals in my small red truck.

The stories in this book are authentic, except one story is pure fiction. It is included to describe how difficult it is to defend one's self against a mortar.

My main purpose for writing this book is to demonstrate that war is about living, breathing people — not just statistics. Many of our war dead have been victims of inept leadership, greed, and megalomaniacs.

I do not dwell on military tactics, objectives, or gore in this book. Instead I share short vignettes that describe specific events about military life on a day-to-day basis. Many funny events took place in the worst places. However, do not be deceived by the humor and playfulness of the men portrayed. They all did their time on the line and were responsible, capable soldiers. At times they were just blowing off steam and felt restless.

I am leaving the graphic, blood and guts war stories to other writers. I prefer to share the trials and tribulations of our guys in a gentle manner, along with some personal photographs to enhance the stories.

DECISIONS

Sometimes the responsibility and decision-making of a leader are mighty hard to take. At the Fonduke Pass, Sarge (the author of this book) had set up his platoon in a wadi (dry stream bed) in the rear of the line. A haggard officer came from the front and demanded to know who was in charge. Sarge admitted to being the Platoon Sergeant. (You do not wear your rank in combat because of snipers, you know.) The officer gave Sarge a direct order that if a straggler came his way and would not return to the front, Sarge was to kill the deserter. This is tough duty. We all hate deserters but to shoot one in cold blood is another matter. All the rest of the day, Sarge hoped that no one would come as he would escort the man back to the front rather than shoot him. He could not ask his men to do this task. Leaders sometimes get a little more money and emoluments — but they sure pay for it.

IT'S A LIVING

During wartime when all hope is lost there is always a perpetual source of income. A girl will spend a few minutes under a young soldier in hopes of receiving a much-desired candy bar, a few lira for pasta or perhaps a little vino to wash it down.

You can plan that the ladies and young girls will generate some funds with their TLC. This happens almost everywhere.

FATHERS

A number of women were huddled around a fireplace near the front line in Italy. A young mother noticed a young Sergeant watching her try to nurse her hungry baby. The little one was squirming and fretting. Suddenly the Sarge produced a small can of American Pet Condensed Milk. He had been saving it for months to make some mouth watering cocoa. He mixed the Pet with some water and then and there changed this baby's formula. The mother fed the formula to her baby and he immediately went into a peaceful sleep.

All of the women and the mother looked at the Sarge with love in their eyes. Until then he had been the enemy. Sarge thought of his two-year-old son back home in the United States whom he had never met.

Young Sarge gave his precious Pet milk to an
Italian mother to feed her hungry baby.

INVASION

A boy sauntered across the beach and noted ships firing at his island.
He climbed up the hill to his home where he had resided for about twelve
years. As he reached the house, a large naval shell hit and pulverized
him. Animals and birds came to the feast. The next morning the assault
troops came up the hill and there was no trace of the boy.

BEHIND GERMAN LINES

One very dark night in Tunisia we were moving up to get into position on the line. We traveled all night as the Germans had air superiority and controlled the roads during the day. Our troopies were well-trained and observed strict night movement procedure. We did not rev our trucks but rolled along as quietly as possible — there was no smoking or lights. Our vehicle lights were cats' eyes and were little dots of blue. Sometimes we wore white winter gear and walked in front of the vehicles so the driver could follow the guide and stay on the road.

Sarge was never completely comfortable waltzing along the road in a white coat. We traveled what seemed like hours and came to a railroad crossing with a flagman's hut. Two British soldiers challenged us. They asked if the big push was on as we were many miles behind the German lines and must be attacking. After a hurried conference, one would have to listen real hard to hear us creeping out of there back to our own lines. We were the "silent army."

CHOW TIME

On the line, the infantryman usually prepared his own meal. If he is lucky it will be "C" rations, which was good ole meat, beans, hash, or stew. "D" rations and British rations are for the birds. One heated the cans in the container the stove was carried in and used the boiling water to make morning coffee. When one man was boiling water a pretty young Italian girl hesitantly put three, honest to goodness, real chicken eggs into the water. The soldier was irate and exclaimed: "Do you know where these eggs came from?" Young Sarge and his first squad leader, Max, knew very well where they came from and agreed to take them. As Sarge and Max consumed the valuable eggs, they agreed that one should never look a gift chicken in the mouth — especially on or near the front line, where eggs are scarce.

POSSESSION,
NOT AS IMPORTANT AS LOVE

Young Sarge came out of the African Campaign with a wonderful German Machine Pistol. It wasn't actually a pistol but a two-handed machine gun. He was proud of it. When he was sent on a Quartering Party from Tunis, Tunisia to Oran, Algeria, he entrusted his precious weapon to his best buddy, First Squad Leader, Max. The Quartering Party established a camp at Oran and the unit came across North Africa. Sarge asked Max for the gun and Max stated that he had a chance to trade the gun for some scarce cigarettes. Sarge asked for his cigs but Max said, "I had to smoke them." This brought up an urge to kill but you don't kill someone you love and on whom you depend to watch your back.

The quartering party set up this attractive bivouac area near Oran, Algeria. There was lots of fresh air and it rained like hell. A pup tent is not very comfortable. If you touch the canvas it will start to leak. Anyway, it's home sweet home.

Rocky Ridge Resort near Oran

OUR MASCOT PETE

Pete was the mascot and darling of AT Company, 133rd Infantry, 34th Division Iowa National Guard at Camp Claiborne, LA in 1941. Pete was struck by a truck, which fractured his hind leg. In those days when an animal had an injury fracture the animal was usually destroyed. They took Pete to the Guardhouse to have him shot. Young Sarge was Sergeant of the Guard that day. Sarge issued to himself some real (not guard special) ammo. He put Pete into a Jeep and they headed for the rifle range, a legal place to discharge firearms. Sarge and Pete eyeballed each other and headed for the vet. When the Company was shipped to Europe, someone tossed Pete off the train. A large plaster cast was on his leg.

MOVE 'EM OUT

Young Sarge was moving his platoon forward on a dark night over a narrow road along the side of a mountain in Italy. It was important for the health of the platoon that they reach their position and get dug in before daylight. A French outfit was blocking the road making it impassable. No progress was being made until a Jeep came to a screeching halt. A French Officer leaped from the Jeep, with a riding crop in his hand, screaming bloody murder. He screamed and flailed away at every soldier near him. Miraculously, the road cleared and we were on our way. We can't get away with this kind of behavior in our Army but it is effective.

OBJECTIVE REACHED

The young soldier climbed slowly and laboriously up the mountain in Italy. At the top he hoped the supply guys would find him and give him some food, water, a smoke, and a whole candy bar (seldom seen at the front). As he crawled steadily upward, the sun flashed on the barrel of a sniper's rifle. He no longer had use for the food, water, smoke, or the cherished candy bar.

DESERT MADNESS

This morning before daybreak the young PFC had all the water he could hold and his one canteen was filled to last until evening. As day broke he went to his slit trench, where he had suffered the heat for so many awful days. By noon his canteen was empty and he was experiencing many hallucinations. He thought he heard, "Johnnie, Johnnie, where are you?" He cautiously peeked over the rim of his slit trench. He saw his girl, Tilly, by the cactus field waving for him to come to her. Forgetting his rifle, he rushed to her with arms outstretched. The unit Morning Report for that day began KIA (killed in action), PFC John Doe.

FECOM

The mascot of 2nd Battalion, 38th Infantry, 2nd Division in Korea was named after the Far East Command, thus FECOM. He liked to hang out at the motor pool gate and would climb into the unoccupied rear seat of any Jeep leaving the motor pool. It was not unusual for us traveling around Korea to see our dog zip by in a Jeep belonging to some other outfit. He would change rides until he found his way home. He would hop out of the Jeep and trot over to his dish where he expected to be fed. A spoiled adventurous dog.

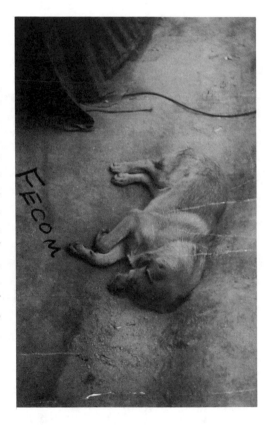

Fecom loved to sightsee around Korea from the rear seat of a Jeep.

SWAMP ANGELS

While on maneuvers in Louisiana some of our guys discovered some very pretty girls. They were a bit wild and some people might classify them as "poor white trash." The whole family lived in a one-room shack. One of our guys had been with one. He would buy a cheap cotton dress and at noon on Saturday after weekly inspection, he would disappear until first call on Monday. He slept with her and the whole family in the one room. We couldn't knock it as he was a happy traveler.

When he left the unit he sold his swamp angel to another guy in the outfit. We didn't mind because it was keeping it in the family.

Sarge was not in the running as he never had enough cash to afford a cheap cotton dress.

BURDICK

We were told to haul ass (retreat) at 1700 hours. We assembled in a cactus patch in the rear. All here? One guy said he saw Burdick rolling wire. Immediately Young Sarge said, "Let's go Smitty," to his driver. They sped down the road toward the Germans and spotted Burdick. As Smitty turned around, Burdick hopped on the running board. All hell was breaking loose and we were up to our asses in Germans. We got Burdick back all safe and sound. Nobody said, "Good job!" to Sarge and Smitty; not even a "Thank you" from Burdick. You really have to do something brave to get a pat on the back from this outfit. Burdick went on to become a Lieutenant Colonel in the Infantry.

A 2½ ton truck used by Smitty and Sarge to go get Burdick from the Germans.

BILLY

Young Sarge and his platoon were shooting the bull near a large sturdy farm building in Italy. A barrage surprised us and we headed for safety behind this fortress-like building. Billy froze and could not move a muscle. Young Sarge dashed out and pulled him into relative safety. No one said a word. Sarge was expected to do things like this. A man has to do what a man has to do.

Billy working on the duck boards after a heavy rain. It was a long time until Sarge dragged him in from another rain of hot metal.

THIEVES

When the Company boarded the troop ship in Oran, North Africa for the invasion of Italy the outfit was in poor condition. Each man carried everything he owned in a little drawstring "B" bag. Some might have had one set of underwear, but most had their souvenirs, which they had taken from some reluctant German and Italian soldiers. The crew said to leave the bags in one compartment and they would guard them for us. We did enjoy the overnight trip with no guard duty. We had hot food, hot coffee and a real bunk to stretch out on. As we were going over the side to board the landing craft we were busy and confused. We had never gone down the nets before. Stukes hit the ship next to us. It burned like hell. Things were going off all over the place. In these exciting times we did not realize that our little bags were all empty. Our own Navy robbed us of our German Lugers, P-38s, machine pistols, Berettas, bayonets, flags, etc. All precious to us. If we had known earlier, chances are some of my unstable guys would have begun the invasion right on the ship.

The only satisfaction we could feel was that the crew was not trained in ground warfare and would probably shoot the hell out of each other.

CLEARING A SANITORIUM

While moving up in Northern Italy the Lieutenant (Lt.) drove Sparky and Sarge into a courtyard of a sanitorium in bright moonlight. He said, "You and Sparky clear this building, while I go back and get the rest of the platoon." Now Sparky was special. He blew a bugle in some military school and so was commissioned. He was not the soldier type. He strutted around with this big ole hogleg strapped to his waist. Each Platoon Sergeant had to babysit him on a sort of schedule. I agreed to take him if he would man the radio all night — which he seemed to enjoy.

We had to climb up three stories of long steps to reach the top floor. As we cleared each floor of this spooky place Sarge used the proper procedure. He kicked open the door, looked through the crack, then cautiously peeked around the doorjamb. When Sarge peeked in he felt pressure on his back. When he realized it was Sparky's hogleg he almost jumped out of his skin.

If one thing had startled ole Sparky, Sarge was a dead man. Sarge snatched the pistol from Sparky and gave Sparky his carbine. From then on as they peeked in each door, Sarge could look down and see the barrel of the carbine. Except for a possible enemy, Sarge felt a lot safer.

THE FART

The outfit had just captured a fort-like, walled town. We were standing and admiring a well-dug slit trench, dug by a German soldier in the farmyard. We were tense as we knew the enemy would try to take back what they had lost.

When Dan let out a fart that sounded a lot like an incoming shell, Inky jumped into the trench. After we all laughed we forgot about it.

A short time later a few of us were crowded around a small fire in a shepherd's hut. Dan said that it was boring in the hut and he should provide some entertainment. He would fart and Inky would dive to the floor. Instead Inky dove on ole Dan.

It was no longer boring. It was lively 'til Sarge got them quieted down. Bet every German wondered what the hell the Americans were up to.

SNOOKERED

Young Sarge was observing through a slit in the shutters, watching German artillery explode over a field between his position and the first squad. The shells contained some interesting propaganda leaflets. They hoped to catch our guys out there collecting these leaflets. They would wait until dark and then throw a heavy barrage on the area.

Sarge figured that if he crossed at twilight he would make it. He ran out and was stuffing the leaflets into his shirt when the Germans started firing early and snookered him. He dove into a shallow irrigation ditch and dug in with his belt buckle. The concussion rolled him over and he was looking up at the stars. This happened a few times and he had had enough of this crap so he broke for the squad position. As he entered the barnyard he tripped over a trail spike. He could have won an Olympic medal for the longest run-hop-leap contest.

He limped into the house and there sat his buddy, Max. He said, "Max, they almost got me this time." Max wasn't impressed and replied, "You always say that." The urge to kill was strong but Sarge was too mad, his leg hurt too much, and he had had the crap scared out of him.

Happy Days Gone

Young Sarge knew that Nazi propaganda was a lot of baloney. But when "Happy Days Gone" was shot over by the Germans it gave him time to reflect.

For months on end he had not slept or eaten well, had no good drinks, and absolutely no safe entertainment.

Some guys, a few hundred yards away, were constantly trying to change his lifestyle by killing him. Yes, he paused to reflect — just what the hell am I doing here?

ZYCHECK

Zycheck was a mountain of a man from Minnesota and the Platoon Sergeant of our Mine Platoon. These Sergeants were responsible for discovering and destroying enemy mines — a dangerous business.

Once while removing a mine, Zy set off a second mine that the Germans had set as a booby trap. As the medics were carrying him off, he was heard to exclaim, "One damn fine war — but oi what a muzzle blast!"

For their own information the medics counted the lacerations on his body. There were over 400, some sort of record. He returned to us and was KIA in Italy.

11

WOCHECK

Wocheck was another monster of a man from Minnesota.

We lived in small, company-sized camps that were scattered all over Northern Ireland. There wasn't much entertainment so we went to a small dance hall in Moy.

Wo wanted to go to the dance on Saturday night. Young Sarge was the only one who knew how to dance so Wo ordered him to be the teacher. Wo had two left feet. As this monster was mauling the 130-pound Sarge around the barracks, the Old Man walked in and didn't want to believe what he was seeing. Sarge convinced him that Wo and Sarge were not an item and that Sarge was teaching Wo the Box Step.

Wo went to the dance and danced with a lively Irish lass.

Wo received a Field Commission as a Second Lieutenant in one of the Ranger Battalions. He was KIA, leading his unit in Sicily. He was one of the bravest men Sarge has ever known.

KEPPIE

Keppie Kephart was the smallest man in the outfit. He wasn't pretty but he was lovable. Every payday we'd join the crap game and contribute to the cool guys. For over two years he contributed every month.

Once in a game out in the desert, Young Sarge lost all of his money. He lay down in the sand and went to sleep. When he awoke in the morning there was Keppie matching his winnings. We had fourteen kinds of money in the game: pounds, francs, lira, dollars, invasion money, and other money from countries in North Africa. The North African money was printed on poor grade paper and tore apart easily. Keppie was matching this paper and using medical tape to hold it together.

After the war I saw Keppie at a reunion in Sioux City, Iowa. He said he often thinks of the time that he was a rich sheik in the Sahara Desert in Tunisia, North Africa.

CHET AND HIS GALOSHES

The Company had moved out of Casino and was en route to the Anzio Beachhead. This was like going from the frying pan into the fire.

While being briefed on landing and moving inland in a hurry, the Old Man (Company Commander) stated that we would be moving fast so no galoshes would be authorized. Sgt. Chet stood up and stated that if he did not wear galoshes he would catch pneumonia!

The Old Man said, "Chet, you will be the only soldier wearing galoshes on the beachhead. Wear them."

There was firing at the port when we arrived so we disembarked and moved out in a hurry. Chet's platoon missed the rear of Sarge's platoon and went up a different street. A faint boom, up near Rome and Anzio Annie, the gigantic cannon, had sent a round on the way. It lit on the intersection that Chet's platoon was crossing.

In a picture of the incident in *Life* magazine we could tell the dead Sergeant was Chet because of the galoshes. Chet would rather have contracted pneumonia.

Keppie, Sarge and Doretta at a rest camp at the Arlington Hotel in Hot Springs, Arkansas. Keppie had already spent his money and was no longer a "rich sheik of the desert."

13

RECON

Moving up for the attack on the fortress town of Casino, the Ole Man needed to know how he would get the unit through the town of Chevero. The road to the town was in good condition, but we had to get through the town before daybreak and into a fairly secure bivouac area. He called Young Sarge and Sgt. Zycheck to make the recon. They started out during the darkness and as daylight broke they traveled in gullies and shallow valleys. Coming down out of one of the valleys they spotted a pretty, small, undamaged church. As they entered the church they saw, stacked to the ceiling, coffins of civilians killed in bombing and artillery from both sides. This was old hat, but a scene on an altar was shocking. A wag had placed a beautiful young girl on an altar, spread her legs, and pulled her dress above her knees. She would never have consented to this if she were alive. Sarge could not hold back the tears.

Later Sarge told his wife. When he was stationed in Germany he took her down there to the church. It was an unhappy time for them as his wife's brother had been KIA a short distance from there during our attack on Casino. Sarge can close his eyes and see the girl as if it were yesterday. The recon was a success and we met the unit at the edge of town and led the way through without incident.

Zy took this picture while he and Sarge were on a reconnaissance mission to find a truck route through the town of Chevero, Italy.

14

GOING HOME

Young Sarge had the highest IQ in the Company. This might explain the many projects to which he was assigned. When he was sent to the rear with battle fatigue his service record was unavailable. To set up a new record, he was required to take an IQ test. The fact that he tested as an "idiot" may explain why he acts as he does.

He claimed, "People trying to kill you for a long time will certainly lower your score — but will significantly raise your blood pressure."

HOW IT IS IN THE GROUND FORCES

This true story is submitted by an Infantry Platoon Sergeant whose unit, the 133rd Infantry Regiment, 34th Division set a record of 611 days in the line during WWII. In considering the combat readiness of his platoon he did not concern himself with things like bread (sometimes fresh), ice cream, hot food, coffee, soda waters, a decent place to eat or where his bunk would be that night. In the short run, he was concerned with the following:

HUNGER!   Will they get three meals up to us tomorrow?
Will they at least be warm?

THIRST!   Sure will be glad when it gets dark and they can get the water up to us. This one canteen a day sucks.

HEALTH!   When are we going to be relieved out of effective range of rifles, artillery, ncbclwerfers, snipers, mines, booby traps, Messerschmitts, Folk Wolff's, friendly artillery and friendly air attacks so that I can get enough water to clean up these filthy troopies?

REST!   Guess it's time that I check security and find a secure place to lie down. It's cold out tonight and there is no place to go to get warm.

PATTON

General Patton spent a lot of time at the front, which didn't please us that much. You could bet that he would draw fire and then haul ass. Other high-ranking officers joined him so it looked like a herd of elephants coming across the desert. His vehicles raised dust. The Germans loved shooting into a cloud knowing that some GIs were bound to be in the vicinity. As the General left, Sarge did a beautiful swan dive into any defilade. He visited us in Italy and we appreciated that he transferred to France. He lost a lot of favor with us "ground-pounders" when he slapped a young soldier at a hospital in Sicily. Many of us have seen men crack up when subjected to a barrage. They shake and cannot stop. Sarge has done the ole shake-rattle-and roll a few times — a man has to dance when he hears the music.

TO THE VICTORS GO THE SPOILS

When you take a town from the enemy it becomes your very own shopping mall. Everything is free. It was interesting to roam through homes when the owners were away. We did not loot too much as we did not have transport. German soldiers were good "shoppers" and they sent all the good stuff to the north. The Italians tried in any way they could to hide their stuff. They hid small cars under haystacks and Singer sewing machines in the wells. Anything that not hidden went to Germany.

Jake shopped up an elegant gramophone with heavy brass or copper discs. He carried it into the street and turned it on. He leaned against a tree, drank from a bottle of vino and listened to the great Caruso. Then the damn thing blew up and spoiled his entertainment. Guess the German troopie who booby-trapped this machine was not a fan of Caruso. He was probably a fan of Lili Marlene.

Jake relaxed against one of these trees when his gramophone exploded.

CHICINA

Our Company reluctantly moved into the center of Chicina. We knew the Germans would be back in one form or another. Sure enough, in the early evening, the Luftwaffe strafed every street and cross street. We cowered in the stairwells and watched them go by — tracers and all.

Our First Soldier called all of the Platoon Sergeants together for a meeting. He unveiled an enormous demijohn of white wine and stated that we would be feeling no pain when the Germans returned. They always returned to raise a little more hell.

We became so "wine brave" that we climbed up on the roof and cheered them on. I can still hear the Old Man chewing our asses out. His total brain trust was on the roof — veterans of North Africa and the long hard fight up to the boot of Italy. He never put us in the center of any more towns and we never pulled that crap again.

TODDY

Young Sarge is now old Lieutenant (Lt.), a Field Commission in Korea. He was assigned to Hq Co, 2nd Bn, 38th Inf, 2nd Division in Korea. The Division was dug in on the General Outpost in the Chorwan Valley. There were about a million Chinese across from them so it behooved them to stay alert. They did routine patrolling, electronic surveillance and inspections at night to make sure that the guards were awake and alert. Battalion officers were placed on rosters and some would go out every night. The O (officer) would report to the S3 shack and be shown where to go that night. Lt. would get his assignment and stop by the mess for a couple of snorts of medicine — it's cold in Korea at night. The driver would take Lt. up as far as he could and Lt. would continue on foot. He would check in with the ground unit and if unsure where to locate a specific outpost the unit would furnish a guide. The outposts were usually two soldiers. He would never sneak up on them as it was dark and spooky out there, and the GI's were usually trigger happy.

That night he found two small black boys at the outpost guarding the whole U.S. Army. Two Chinese kids were doing the same thing a few yards up the ridgeline, guarding the Chinese Army. Our guys were lonely so Lt. sat on the lip of the trench and they had a good bull session. When he left, he always asked what he could do for them. His eyes misted a bit when one asked for more Toddy, a chocolate drink they received when the PX supplies got up to them. Lt. promised Toddy. The next morning he went to the Regimental PX Officer and ordered a case of Toddy to be delivered to the little guys. And it was.

JESSIE

When we arrived in Africa, we were briefed that the Arabs were at least eighty percent pro-Nazi, and if we were caught by the Arabs they would do horrible things to us. They would sever our testicles and sew them in our mouths. With this knowledge our treatment of Arabs caused the number to rise to close to one hundred percent.

Moving up to the line in Tunisia, we passed through many small Arab villages with residents standing along the road watching us. At the end of each village, Sarge would hear a commotion. He turned around to observe what was causing it. Sarge saw Jessie riding the trails of a 37mm anti-tank gun. Trails are used to pull the gun and to steady it when you fire. The gun crew in the truck would coax the villagers to come closer to the truck. Jessie would come along with a broom and knock the hell out of them. This is no way to increase our popularity in the country so Sarge put ole Jessie in the truck and spoiled his fun game. Sarge bets that the Arabs would have liked to chop off Jessie's nuts.

Jessie used to create fear in the hearts of the enemy.

The trail that ole Jessie was riding as he knocked the hell out of the Arabs. It takes a little balancing act to keep from dismounting.

MILK

The farmers in Italy usually had cow barns attached to their kitchens. Sarge peeked out the kitchen door and couldn't believe his eyes. Here was the most beautiful cow he had ever seen. The farmers usually took all livestock with them when they hid in the hills. We liked to eat them, and so did the Germans, who took everything. Being an ole, part-time farm boy, Sarge knew the cow needed milking as all of her faucets were dripping. We doubted that the cow was booby trapped so Sarge started to milk her. Suddenly the whole outfit wanted to milk. I think they just wanted a lot of warm titty in their hands. It was a long time since they had been close to real females.

ATROCITY

About this time Sarge had hit a low point in his Dago Red Vino Consumption. At dusk the Lt. and Sarge pulled up in front of an imposing building. Sarge thought it was a winery so when the Lt. said to clear it and he would be back with the outfit, Sarge knew where to search for enemies. In the basement there were gigantic barrels of wine. He was jubilant until he noticed that some undisciplined German GI had shot into the barrels and allowed the beautiful Dago Red to drain into the gutter. For months the Germans had been trying to kill him and he had never hated them. Until now. Now he thought the Germans should be shot for perpetuating this atrocity.

19

MORTAR

In the flat desert of Tunisia our artillery had to stay way back for concealment. They could not reach the front line to give protection from enemy armor. Their tankers would park out there with impunity and fire at will. Our Old Man sent the Supply Sergeant to the rear to obtain a couple of 81mm mortars. Young Sarge and another man had been in the old Howitzer Company and had trained with the old WWI Stokes Mortar. They set up the mortars and managed to poop a couple of rounds toward the enemy. When the enemy tank commanders saw the mortars they cranked up and hauled ass. A mortar shell landing on the top can give one a hell of a headache. It shakes up the crew and may cause a fire. Hoorah for Yankee ingenuity.

WWI Stokes Mortar. Sarge trained on this weapon in the 1930s and used the knowledge to drive off tanks in Tunisia in 1943.

RECREATION

We pulled up in front of an impressive building. The Lt. told Sarge to check it out and that he would be back with the outfit. Sarge checked out two floors and then made a beeline for the basement. He knew where the vino was stored. Lo and behold, he discovered enormous barrels of real ole Dago Red. He also found a most beautiful bedroom. After checking the bed for booby traps, he leaped onto the bed to test it. He got his canteen cup out and headed for the barrels. A pleasant evening was in store. As he headed out the door he heard his buddy Max shout, "Sarge we're moving out!"

How can a soldier stand this kind of disappointment?

BAZOOKA

In Tunisia we stood to every morning. The Germans preferred to attack from the east with the sun at their backs and it gave them a whole day of daylight to attain their objectives. We were their greeters, but not too enthusiastic. To stop their armor the Old Man acquired some bazookas. They look like a piece of poorly designed plumbing. It was designed to hurl a large rocket. It was effective when we learned how to operate it.

Even if you didn't get a direct hit, it was good at discouraging a tank from remaining in your neighborhood. Sarge assigned the plumbing to himself as everyone else had a job. He dug a trench for it next to his own slit trench and was ready to destroy the German tank corps. Tanks did not come and the Company was ordered into reserve.

Sarge decided to demonstrate the plumbing. There was a tremendous bang, the rocket took off and destroyed a target. Sarge looked like he had a severe case of small pox. What they didn't tell him was that burned rocket fuel was hot and harmful. It seems that the face mask and asbestos gloves had not been issued with the plumbing. No medal was authorized for rocket burn. Sarge made up his mind then and there that if the Old Man brought up any more weapons he would not volunteer to test them. He would cajole ole Max into doing it.

MINES

The Supply Sergeant issued each man a metal container about the size of a thick fiction book. He explained that if a tank came near, you were to fling it under one of the two treads. This will immobilize the tank and it will no longer be an effective fighting machine. Infantry men are not the smartest guys on the straus (street), but we are not stupid. Who in his right mind would stop a behemoth on top of his slit trench or fox hole? For us this weapon became obsolete and not to be used in any sense. When we went into reserve we found that the box had to be armed with a fuse, which were in an officer's pocket on the other side of the hill.

Can you imagine anyone stupid enough
to stop one of these on top of his fox hole?

SOMBITCH

On a long monotonous convoy trip, Sarge amused himself at the expense of German youth. As the convoy wound through a village, the youths yelled, "Chum gum!" (for chewing gum). Soldiers threw pieces of gum to them. Sarge found that if he counted the kids and threw one less piece than the total, he could cause a mini riot. If you were lucky, you could leave the village with every kid in a fight. If you did not throw any candy or gum, they would call you, "Sombitch!" (for son-of-a-bitch).

YUGLI-LI

Every unit on the line or General Outpost in Korea was assigned a village in the rear for moral and supply support. Our village, Yugli-li, was about a three hour drive south. Sarge as Lt. S4 (supply officer) was assigned as chief honcho for this operation. He had a meeting with the Head Man of the village and determined that school supplies were most essential. Lt. asked the troopies to write home for donations. The response was amazing. Everything from fruit to nuts was sent — even dress shirts, shoe ice-skates, lots of candy, puzzles, clothing and of course lots of school supplies. Distribution was made at the school. Headmaster distributed the school supplies. Mamasans made a huge stew from the food. Village elders distributed the clothing according to the needs of each family. Each troopie kind of adopted a kid. We planned another party when more GIs could join us.

Yugli-Li.
January 6, 1954

CASBAH

The Casbah was surrounded by Military Police (MPs); they didn't want you in there. Too many of our guys had been injured there. Not to be denied entry, Sarge hired a monstrous black man to carry him and whomever was traveling with him and Max. They were roaming around like kings of the hill when the MP patrol caught up with them. The MPs were not upset to find us in there. They just showed us their bloody hands from hauling the last batch to the emergency room. Never missing a beat, Sarge jumped in the Jeep and exclaimed, "Come on guys! We finished our business in here." And we rode peacefully to safety.

DANCE

We took some of our soldiers who had kids of their own for a party at the school we sponsored in Yugli-li, Korea. The dance teacher gave a recital of Korean folk dancing. The only furniture in the school room was a tiny organ. The little girls were charming and graceful. The only difference in their dance was that due to wartime shortage they did not have handkerchiefs. They would slide gracefully to a stop, wipe their noses on the sleeves of their beautiful costumes and continue on with the dance. It was step, stop, sniff and continue with the routine.

One little girl danced while wiping her runny nose on the sleeve of her pretty costume.

LATRINES

While visiting our school in Yugli-li, Korea we noticed the students defecating in an open slit trench just like soldiers do. We decided to construct a sanitary sit-down privy. Our carpenter did himself proud. He constructed the greatest three holer you've ever seen. We presented it to the village Head Man with pride and proper ceremony. Some time later we visited the school and it was back to the open trench for the students. It seems that our beautiful three holer was a spreader of diseases — diseases that could reach the kids as they sat and chatted.

American ingenuity foiled again.

Headmaster and his staff
at Yugli-li School.

Little girls playing yard games
— just like back home.

Whole class at
Yugli-li School.
January 1954

The kids were orderly as
W.O. Canada gives out candy.

26

When the Headmaster blew an assembly whistle the students immediately went to their places in line and stood quietly.

BARTER

Moving up in Tunisia, Sarge stopped his Jeep by an Arab who had a real egg. Sarge hadn't had a real egg in months and really wanted this one. The only things he had to trade were English cigarettes, Players Please — a terrible cig, all weeds, little tobacco.

The Arab took his time scrutinizing the cigs and asked for "Camel" cigarettes. Sarge hadn't had an American cigarette in months. Sarge went berserk, grabbed his rifle from the boot on the Jeep and tried to shoot the Arab. His driver wrestled with him and shouted that if he shot once we'd be up to our asses in Arabs; they would come out of the woodwork (desert) and we'd be in deep poop. Sarge then developed a procedure. His driver would slowly pass by the Arab, Sarge would reach out, snatch the egg and they would race off. There were some pissed off Arabs!

SEWING BEE

At Hill 609 (the last great battle before we took the city of Tunis, Tunisia), Sarge was hit in the head by a large rock. It's a good thing that he is a Swede or it could have been serious. We all know that Swedes are hardheaded.

They drove him back to an aid station for sewing. They put him on a stretcher, balanced on two med travel cases.

A poker game was in progress on the floor in the corner of the tent. As Doc would take a stitch, someone would raise a quarter, which was a large sum in those days. Doc would stop sewing and peer at this interesting game. He would continue sewing until the next bet and then peer again.

Boy was Sarge happy when someone won the hand. They stuck Sarge in a Jeep, the Medic Colonel put his coat around Sarge's shoulders and off they went for the front. The Jeep pulled up in front of a pup tent, the driver snatched the coat from Sarge, and Sarge was left for a hell of a night with a bodacious headache.

War is hell.

LADIES FIRST

When an Arab family went down the road, the head of household always came first and mama came last. Papa would go along kicking the mule in the belly so that it would remember to keep on trucking.

Wartime changes many customs and so in this war the ladies were permitted to go first. This all happened because the Germans had the nasty habit of placing land mines in the road to deny us safe passage. A number of times we have seen Arabs go up a road, a mine would be tripped and the procession would panic and start to scatter. Thus more and more devices would be set off, creating a slaughter.

Our Old Man would never let us help. With all this confusion we would also become casualties. The Old Man sat on his donkey knowing that he had an efficient mine sweeper out in front. We lost a lot of guys to mines and booby traps.

Since the Germans started to mine the roads,
ladies were permitted to walk in front.

NEW ORLEANS BRIDE

At Camp Claiborne, Louisiana the guys were always getting into strange situations when they were on pass. Our Mess Sergeant came back with the story of his experience in New Orleans. He claimed that he got drunk one Saturday night, woke up in a seedy hotel room, the ceiling fan barely moving and with a terrible hangover headache. When he realized he was sleeping between two enormous black women, he wanted out of there. He cautiously crawled over one lady and she opened her eyes and said, "Not me honey. I'se de bridesmaid." A likely story.

THE GENERAL'S TRAILER

Down in the Tunisian desert one of our Sergeants came into camp proudly pulling a beautiful trailer he had captured. When the Old Man saw it, he ordered the Sergeant to take it out in the desert and bury it. The Sergeant had inadvertently acquired the Commanding General's trailer. Guess the Old Man thought there was no way to explain this so he hid it. Bet ole General is still wondering what the hell happened to his trailer.

LEMON EXTRACT

Max and his buddies were on their way to a dance in Portadown, Northern Ireland. They needed a few drinks for the night. A bottle of Irish whiskey cost a whole pound ($4.25), which was a lot of money in those days. They went to the Mess Sergeant, a buddy, and mooched a bottle of lemon extract. At that time the Army issued 150 proof vanilla and lemon extract. The vanilla wasn't too bad but we had to make sure that we never got near the Old Man as we'd smell like a fruit cake.

The lemon extract tasted terrible even when mixed in a soda water. When having a drink we would keep our bottle under the table and mix extract with a Irish soda, called Tutti-Frutti, for our girls. To our amazement they smacked their lips and enjoyed the drink. We figured that being in the war zone for so long, they wouldn't recognize the crap we served them. Regardless of what I put in the extract it made all my ends pucker.

PRISONERS

While attacking off the Anzio Beachhead toward Rome we set up security when we stopped for the day. We selected a large and long cave. We set up security and Sarge and another soldier guarded one end. They heard sounds from around the bend in a stream that continued on through the cave. They took prone positions on each side of the opening. A German soldier peeked at them from around the bend. Sarge waved for him to come forward but his head disappeared.

We heard some more noise and figured the Germans were finishing their rations. They knew that prisoners were not fed until interrogation. Hungry men tend to be a little more chatty. Two very young soldiers came out. Sarge was only twenty-one years old, so you know ole Hitler was reaching the bottom of the barrel to use such young fighters as these. We were tempted to send them to "the happy soldier hunting ground" but we just couldn't kill these youngsters. Here we were with two gray uniformed soldiers between us and our guys.

To solve this dilemma we sang loudly as we sloshed through the water. Smitty got one of their watches. One guy gave out pictures that were taken in Paris. Sarge still has his. He is still glad that they spared those young soldiers.

Sarge and his buddy captured this soldier near Villa Cuesilla Anzio Beachhead on May 3, 1944

Sarge and a buddy captured one of these guys.

31

MASH

Sarge and one of his troopies were observing through a hole in the roof of a cave when a barrage blanketed the hole. They were not wounded but concussion made them a little goofy. They were hauled to a MASH hospital to sleep it off.

After the first restful night of sleep in months, Sarge awoke to a Hawkeye type doctor who patted him on the stomach and asked if his tummy hurt. Nobody had been kind to Sarge for a long time and he had a hard time handling it. The doctor asked if there was anything that he could do for Sarge. Sarge asked for a shot of real American whiskey. The doctor left and a pretty nurse came back with the shot.

Sarge downed the shot and the nurse handed him a message to report back to his unit. This was a short but pleasurable rest camp.

GIBBS

It was Gibbs' and Sarge's turn to leave the nest and bring up the rations. Rations were delivered to the rear-most position. They were called "10-in-1s" — rations for ten men for one day. Usually we were not too hungry in defense and there was some stuff we just didn't eat. We went along the large irrigation ditches so we could jump in for protection if necessary.

Axis Sally, broadcasting from Rome, informed us that there was beer on the wharves in Naples and that we would get some soon. To our delight and amazement there was beer. Three large bottles went to our position. We loaded a sandbag with beer and packed food in two other bags.

On the way back to our position a German round went over. No problem. Another fell short. Big problem. We knew the next one would be right in there. It's called "ranging." Gibbs said they hit the canal. Sarge wrapped around Gibbs with the beer between them. The groceries sat on the pathway. Gibbs claims that Sarge was more concerned with the beer than his health.

DECEMBER 7th, 1941

It was Sunday night and the guys in camp were almost bedded down in anticipation of an arduous week of training. A call came down for all Non-Commissioned Officers (NCOs) to report to the Orderly Room. The Company Commander (CO) announced that we were moving out for New Orleans at 0200 (Two o'clock in the morning).

We were to break camp, put all items not needed on the move into the mess hall, including the canvas tent frame covers. We were all ready to go when we discovered that there were insufficient drivers for our vehicles. Regardless of whether or not they had ever driven, some guys with lots of guts were recruited. An NCO driver would follow each of the volunteers. When it seemed as if a driver had fallen asleep the NCO would close up on him, honk the horn, and raise hell until he awoke. Mercifully all vehicles made it to Lake Ponchartrain, just north of New Orleans. We listened to our President declare war on Japan. We were ordered to Norco, LA on sabotage duty — and thus the war began for us.

The trucks we managed to get to New Orleans.

NORCO, LA

Shortly after the President's speech the unit was ordered to an oil refinery at Norco, LA to prevent espionage. It was like going home — the populace welcomed us with open arms. We became a part of their community. Many guys were invited to home-cooked meals, many dated the lovely girls (Southern Belles, that is).

There were not enough boys to go around to escort the senior girls to the prom, so young guys like Sarge escorted the girls. This was real good duty. Sarge was amazed that there was a full service bar in the gym. Many free drinks were offered but the guys behaved themselves for the most part and did not over imbibe. Lucas went back and married one of the Belles.

When we left for Europe it was just like the night we marched out of our hometown — Sioux City, Iowa. Each one in the unit received a gift of a flat-fifty of cigarettes, which most of us could not afford. During most of our hard duty in combat in Africa and Italy we never forgot Norco.

DANGEROUS SHOWER

Anzio was like a bad dream. The battle lasted for four months — it was hell. During these four months, the Allies suffered over 29,000 combat casualties. German casualties were estimated at 27,000.

To shower one had to take the chow truck to the rear at night and come back up the line the following night. It was said that the Germans could land an artillery shell on a blanket-sized area anywhere on the beachhead. Thus it was very dangerous to shower in the open — even if you were out of the line-of-sight. Sarge tried it once. This was his one and only shower in four months.

WILLY

At the Hohenfels Training Camp in West Germany, Captain Willy took exception to something that ole Cap had said when he was being obnoxious, "Take your best shot, Willy!" Then Cap stuck his chin out.

Damned if ole Willy didn't take a shot. Cap got up off the floor and was obliged to teach Willy some manners by beating the crap out of him. As Cap left the room, Willy stated that he would shoot ole Cap.

Cap knew that ole Willy had fought many battles in WWII and Korea, so he did the better part of valor and sought protection from his troopies. He went down to their quarters and told the Charge-of-Quarters (CQ) that under no circumstances was Willy to get near. Feeling no fear, sleeping among his soldiers, Cap had a good night's sleep. Peace was made the next morning, but ole Cap always kept his eye on Willy. Surveillance is most of the game.

OFF LIMITS

On the front line in Africa, Arabs were forbidden to cross. If they did not go back they were killed. We learned this from an unfortunate experience. We had noticed a solitary Arab walking near a single white hut on a cliff across from our positions. What we didn't see was the machine gun that he dropped from beneath his large white robe. Later a German gun crew crawled up to the gun and severely shot up our third platoon. Another time we stopped a camel caravan. We found the camels were carrying German mines that we had dug up. They were taking them back to sell to the Germans. Needless to say, the Germans were able to save their money. The front line was off limits.

Arabs were not permitted through our lines as they practiced sabotage.

35

BORDELLO

In reserve when Sarge and Max went somewhere guys wanted to go with them since they always managed to get into some interesting situations. This time Zy and Billy came along. The group came across a house of joy situated on a cliff in Sidi bel Abas, home of the French Foreign Legion. They were denied admittance as the Military Police had declared the place off limits. This is no way to treat guys just off the line for a little excitement. They decided to go over the wall. Max was strong and would cup his hands and on the count of three would toss Sarge on top of the wall. Sarge would pull the others over and surprise the inhabitants. Max gave a bodacious heave and threw Sarge straight above the top of the wall. Sarge looked down and discovered that glass and bottles had been embedded in cement on top of the wall. Sarge pushed off and his butt landed on Max's head. He rode Max's head down to a cobblestone roadway. Imagine Sarge cracking up because this was so funny and it sounded like a watermelon exploding.

BORDELLO NUMBER 2

If these people think they can keep us out of their building, they have another thought coming. Our buddy Max was a little shaken up from our last adventure, so we took him to a bar and filled him full of vino. Max, fully refreshed, led the way to the bottom of the cliff where our objective perched. Looking up, Max discovered a buttress holding up the wall. He scampered up the buttress to a wall that blocked his way. Nearby was a brace protruding from the wall, a little over a yard from the buttress. Max leaped, grabbed the brace and hauled himself over the ledge. This wasn't too difficult for Max as many people mistake him for the missing link. Next Sarge leaped and missed. Max grabbed him and pulled him over the ledge through a million years of pigeon shit. Sarge smelled like pigeon shit but was elated that he made it up to the roof. He called down to Zy and Billy to come on up. They muttered that their mother had not raised any idiots and they refused. Max and Sarge meandered across rooftops until they found a patio where they dropped down into some flower beds. The girls were delighted to see them but told them they could not stay. They showed the boys to a rear door but when they opened the door Zy and Billy rushed in. They all settled into comfortable patio chairs and planned to chat, drink, and perhaps to do a little business. But the MPs pounded on the front door about three stories up. The soldiers had a chance to escape. They ran down a convenient canal and were free. They did not admit defeat. Nothing ventured, nothing gained. Ole Max was in good shape except for a hell of a headache.

Arabs preferred mattress covers for their robes.

MATTRESS COVERS

For some reason we were issued mattress covers in Ireland before we set off for Africa. The covers became cash-on-hand when we reached Africa. It seemed they were perfect for the robes that North Africans wore. The Arabs had screwed us so often that now it was our chance.

When we cut the mattress cover carefully at the seams and folded it loosely it looked like a complete cover. We had tight security as the Arabs were adept at stealing things. When we had one cover to sell, we signaled the "Arab chasers" who would let an Arab through the guard line. We would get our francs and the Arab would be permitted to leave. He would leave, shake out his bargain cover, and start yelling.

Tough luck. The guards would not permit him to come in again. Actually, we were kind. Some of the units would have the guards take back their covers when they tried to leave, which was profit to our side.

OVERCOATS

We arrived in Northern Ireland on the 15th of January. We were the first Army Expeditionary Force (AEF) of all the millions that followed. Our billets were in a housing development that were built by Prince Edward before he abdicated. These were nice, two story, two bedroom family dwellings. About twelve soldiers were housed in each building. There was a wall around the dwellings, which we used as a gate to crawl over if we did not have passes.

We were in a town that we liked — Londonderry. It was perhaps the second largest town in Northern Ireland. It was illegal for our CO to authorize passes every night so we all went over the wall, which was almost 100 percent of the time. We were susceptible to the Irish flu and were required to wear great coats when going to town. The Top Sergeant would make rounds every night. If he caught someone off post without a pass he was OK as long as he was wearing his overcoat. We were getting more exercise climbing over that wall than in our regular PE exercises.

TEA PARTY

During a short period in Tunisia, our artillery could not reach in front of our positions because of concealment problems. It was flat desert. German tank commanders took advantage of this and sat out there plinking away at us with impunity. In case they came across, Sarge's Platoon was sent to reinforce Sid's Platoon. Sarge got his outfit all dug in and ready and went to visit Sid (his brother-in-law). Sid's platoon had just finished dinner, such as it was. Sid had the cooks leave the left over tea. He offered Sarge tea and Sarge couldn't believe it — such hospitality in the middle of the desert. Sid and Sarge sat on the edge of a slit trench and had a good ole fashioned tea party. Sid was KIA — at our attack on Casino, Italy.

Ole Sid has been imbibing another kind of tea. He tries to shoot the top off Zy's bottle.

TOUGH NURSE

When Sarge was sent home, he had to go through the system. First was a visit to the funny farm in the Vatican in Italy. Until then, he had pretty much been king of the hill. Here he got no respect.

When he arrived at the hospital, he walked in and reached in his back pocket for a comb. About a dozen ward boys jumped him because they thought he was a crazed killer.

A little bitty nurse started to boss him around. He politely informed her that he was a combat sergeant and should be treated with respect. But he had time to think about "respect" as he cleaned every latrine in the building.

Later he became friends with the nurse. Late at night they would dance in the laundry room to Glenn Miller tunes.

His grandmother had often told him, "Silence is golden." He practiced this important lesson during the rest of his stay in that hospital.

REST CAMP

When Sarge went into reserve a number of guys would go to rest camp. This one was in Rome. It was only for four days so they really whooped it up.

One morning Sarge and the guys were sleeping it off when the MPs came in and said, "Everybody up! You're going to visit the Pope."

"Sorry," they replied, "But we do not want to visit the Pope."

"Fall in!" the MPs insisted.

So the men straggled up the stairs but planned to escape while marching through Rome. No deal. The MPs were all over the place keeping them in formation.

This might be the only time that Sarge was a little ashamed of the Army. As they crossed St. Peter's Square the British came first in perfect formation. The French likewise and then the Aussies. Finally, they came in, all hung-over and miserable. The MPs stayed with them until they went through the Swiss Guards into the Vatican.

After this visit, however, the men were impressed with the religious pomp and ceremony.

HANDLE BAR HANK

During WWII all liquor products were in short supply. In the little Irish town of Moy there was one bar.

Handle Bar Hank enjoyed being around Americans and always provided an extra ration for us. Three of us — Niscanon, Smitty and Sarge — left the bar in great spirits and began riding our bikes back to camp. We rode up and down a steep hill. It was blackout and there was a narrow road between the hedges. We planned to rush down the hill and coast up and into camp. Unknowingly, three Limey Airmen were coming toward us. Niscanon took off first, peddled madly and barely missed the first Limey. Smitty went next and hit the next Limey head on. Both men were badly hurt and the Limey was later retired from service. The British went to great pains to stick the U.S. with the cost of his retirement.

Sarge took off like a rocket and ran over the whole mess. Niscanon said that Sarge was like a graceful bird that bounced off the blacktop a few times. When he got to Sarge, Sarge was trying to crawl through a hedge with one arm. He had fractured the arm, almost lost one ear and had multiple contusions and scrapes. There was seldom any traffic on country roads at night. Lo and behold, a car came with his blackout on. He took the injured into the American clinic in Moy. From there we were driven to the American hospital in Londonderry. It took the rest of the night to go a short distance because all direction signs had been removed. The British were still expecting an invasion by the Germans.

TOOTH EXTRACTED

In late 1941, our Army was getting our Division ready for deployment overseas. To care for our dental needs the Army embarked on a tooth extraction program. We lined up our company outside the dental clinic and began marching our guys through. Each room in the clinic had two dentist chairs. They would bring our guys in, give them a shot and a note with the time to return to have the tooth extracted. Each person would return five minutes apart.

Sarge went in to his appointed room and showed his note but both chairs were full. The dentist asked, "Sarge, are you tough?"

Sarge answered, "You can bet your ass that I am."

The dentist told him to back up and grab the door knob. Sarge did as he was told and zap — his tooth was out. This process is not recommended but it saves getting in and out of an uncomfortable dentist chair.

FORK

In Africa, in 1943, the American Army met the Africa Corps for the first time. They got a lot of exercise as we allowed them to chase us all over the desert. This phase of dig in, take off and dig again, caused us to lose most of our baggage and supplies.

Sarge wound up with the old type mess kit cover and a precious fork. To make sure he didn't lose the fork, he bent the handle and kept it in his upper right pocket — the live file — over his heart. He was quite willing to lend it to others but kept a sharp eye on the borrower. He expected it to be clean when returned so the borrower would carefully lick off the fork and plunge it repeatedly in the nice clean desert sand. This satisfied Sarge and he put the fork back in his live file — the borrower retained his credit rating.

LIMEY

The Americans were in Ireland for about a year and made friends with members of the British Armed Forces. Sarge and a young Limey became close friends and went out together as often as possible. Sarge knew when his friend had too much to drink because he kept to tradition. At the end of the evening he would stand up, raise his glass and exclaim, "If Nelson had pissed in 'is ale, I would piss in me ale."

So much for tradition.

INKY 2

Sarge and two of his buddies had been in a serious accident and had been taken to the American infirmary in Moy, Northern Ireland. Inky somehow managed to get a ride from Portadown and was looking for a ride to our camp, Derrygally. The Doctor had put Sarge and Mick into an ambulance for transport to the American Hospital in Londonderry. Inky stuck his head in the passenger's side window to ask if the ambulance was going his way. He saw Mick on the lower stretcher and Mick appeared to be dead. Sarge looked at him from the upper stretcher and Sarge was a bloody mess. Inky, who had a habit of snorting, snorted about three times. He said something like, "Oh my God!" He took off at a trot for Derrygally to inform the Charge of Quarters of our problem.

SPONSOR

When a married person is transferred to a unit overseas the unit assigns one of its men as a sponsor. The sponsor takes care of any problems, such as renting a house or lining up transportation.

Our sponsors, Moe and Marcie, met us at the Augsburg train station and took us to our quarters. The next morning they arrived to acquaint us with the area's PX, O Club (Officer's Club), Commissary, etc.

On the way to the autobahn to show us the gasoline station, Marcie (a very proper shy person) took it upon herself to explain the autobahn sign. She said that "fahrt" means to go, "einfahrt" means to enter the autobahn, "ausfahrt" means to leave the autobahn and "friefarht" means to enter and drive on the autobahn. She said that, "With einfahrt, ausfahrt, friefarht, a person really doesn't know which way to fart."

We never let her live this down.

RADIATION

While stationed at the Presidio of San Francisco, ole Lt. was sent to the Navy's ABC School on Treasure Island. "ABC" means atomic, bacteriological, and chemical. Lt. absorbed all he could learn, organized two Atomic Teams at the Presidio and took them to Desert Rock, Nevada to participate in a real live shot (explosion). Morale was high and the troopies were eager to get on with it. The results amazed us. When the bomb exploded, it was so bright that one of our guys claimed that he could see rocks on the floor of our trench through his eyelids. We did intensive training on old shots and returned to the Presidio as a well-trained and experienced team. We continued to train on Saturday mornings. On one mission Lt. hid the source (device) under his Team Sergeant's Jeep seat. Alex traveled all over the Presidio before he found out why the Geiger Counter readings were always so high. To this day, his wife, Polly, thanks Lt. She already had about a dozen kids and believed that Alex's trip, sitting on the source, was a birth control aid.

Best in Parade, Presidio of San Francisco, 1957

CASINO

Our defensive position in Casino was right on the edge of town toward our lines. It was an extremely dangerous place to visit. A German mobile anti-tank weapon would appear at the head of the street, raise hell out in the valley and pull back before we could react. With the help of a tank and about 200 engineers, we worked all night and placed a 57mm anti-tank gun in the front bedroom of a house. If he came again, we had the gun aimed and all we would have to do is crawl up to the gun, hit the trigger and he was ours. The Germans could see the gun so the mobile unit never returned. Needless to say, the Germans broke their backs trying to shell us out of there. It was so rough that two NCOs were required to be there with two other men. Our building was on the south side of a plaza with the Germans holding the north half of the plaza. On guard at night, Sarge would lie in a doorway with his rifle pointed north. One of the other guys would face south guarding his back in case they crept up on us from the rear.

When we first came into this building, there were three massive thick walls between us and the Germans. In their effort to move us out they timed their shelling on the hour and on the half hour — if they missed the hourly shelling. There was one wall remaining when the Old Man told us that the Aussies were relieving us. You could hear a sigh of relief all along the line.

NEW LIEUTENANT

In Casino we always kept a man alert to the north and a man at his back. This night Sarge was guarding out the door and Max was leaning against the wall guarding his back. Sarge heard scraping to the right front of his position. He said, "Halt, who in the hell is out there?"

The person identified himself and answered the password. Sarge told him to come closer. He came closer and Sarge asked him, "What the hell are you doing?" He was a brand new 2nd Lt. who confirmed that he was one of us. He said that Colonel Mitchell had sent him along the line to see if we were alert. Sarge said, "Do you know that half the German Army is just across the street? Get your ass in here. Stay awhile and go back and tell the Colonel that in no way could the line go to sleep."

Every night there had been a nervous German cutting loose with a burp gun. Tonight he must have been in the rear at rest camp. His absence probably saved this young man's life.

MOSQUITO NETS

In Ireland, we were issued mosquito nets and were deliriously happy about it. We heard through the rumor mill that we were going to Africa. The nets sort of clinched it. Ireland was so cold and damp that we liked to imagine warm breezes, palm trees and lovely brown girls serving wine and themselves.

Actually we traveled through the Atlas Mountains, a coastal range along the Mediterranean Sea. It was snowing and bitter cold. We were cold because we were not allowed to put canvas roofs on our vehicles since the Germans had air superiority. We could never tell when they were coming because they would suddenly appear and raise hell.

Max, Mike and Sarge bunked together. They dug a hole a few inches deep, put a pup tent over the hole and prepared to retire. We laid one blanket on the ground, wrapped our boots in the mosquito net, snuggled up and pushed our heads up into the dirt bank. With the other two blankets it was as warm and toasty as home. Americans are so adaptive.

NCO CLUB

On the General Outpost in the Chorwon Valley, South Korea, the CO of the 2nd Bn, 38th Infantry decided that our rifle company sergeants were doing such a terrific job that we would reward them. About the only thing one can do for an infantryman is to give him more grief. It is difficult to reward him.

The Colonel decided that we would organize an NCO Club at the Battalion Headquarters. We would send a 2½ ton truck each evening to round them up and then take them home. We pitched a big squad tent, stocked it with spirits and anything we could find to sit on. Rule number one was that all weapons had to be checked at the door.

Everything went smoothly for a few weeks until that fateful night that we closed the Club. One very drunk sergeant couldn't see a place to sit on the truck so he tried to shoot one guy off to make room for himself. After a big fight, we locked the door (so to speak).

SOUVENIRS

All property taken from the enemy belongs to our employer, the U.S.A. The Commanding General of our Division ordered that all souvenirs taken by members of the Division were the personal property of the individual. The souvenirs could be turned in to and stored by the supply sergeant and picked up upon leaving the Division. From then on, the individual was on his own.

Souvenirs could be a source of income when taken away from reluctant enemies — a dangerous occupation, for sure. U.S. Navy personnel were excellent customers as they had money. These wares had to be taken to a seaport because Naval personnel were not going to come to the line to barter. However, there was one serious problem with these customers. They would show the souvenirs to our replacements and tell them horrible stories of how they captured them. Our replacements were scared shitless before we got them up on the line.

Sarge sold two matching 44s and a P-38 to a civilian ship Captain for $25 and a carton of cigarettes. Cap knew that Sarge had to sell these items because if he were caught with them in the U.S. he would be sent back.

T/Sgt — Military Science Faculty
St. Marys University, 1947

46

VEHICLES

When the Germans retreated from North Africa, they tried to destroy all of the vehicles that they were unable to take with them. They destroyed as many as they could but some fell through the cracks.

Our GIs were in Seventh Heaven when they acquired anything with wheels. However, they caused so many injuries and deaths that the vehicles were declared off limits and we were to confiscate them. We got all but one in our unit. Slim, an ole mountain boy, had an enormous 3 ton truck that ditched out. We never found it. He would hide it and walk miles back to camp. Guess he sold it before we moved to Oran.

The Transportation Sergeant found a nice Ford or Chevy roadster in fair condition. His crew fixed it up. Somehow they fitted Jeep tires on it. They jumped in and went for a ride. They stopped at a bar for a cool drink, came out and someone had stolen the car. This goes to show that we couldn't trust the Arabs or Americans. The Germans had all sizes of motorcycles. Sid had an enormous cycle. While we were basking under a canvas sunshield, ole Sid in his cups came racing by waving and shouting greetings. He didn't notice the six-foot dirt bank in front of him. He hit the bank and set some kind of soaring record. He hit some sand but was not injured too badly. We all cheered him on. His cycle was now junk.

This tracked motorcycle could go almost anyplace.

Germans used many horses to pull artillery.

47

The German prime mover pulled their heavy artillery.
It could haul the gun crew in the comfortable seats.

Sarge in a VW scout car. It had balloon tires and
could scoot across the desert. It was hard to hit.

SARGE'S .50

In Africa, Sarge noticed a nice 3/4 ton truck with a .50 caliber machine gun and mount standing unattended along the road. He sent his Transportation Corporal to see if he could help fix it. The next morning we spruced up our truck and laid down some ground rules.

An air attack is horrible because you don't know where to go or what to do. It's best to keep busy. In an air attack the first person to the gun was the gunner. The next person must reluctantly stay as loader. Sarge set up his bunk in the bed of the truck and thus he was the first one there — so he got to shoot most of the time. This was great sport. The guys confirmed that he got at least one plane.

We had spent countless hours in aircraft identification while in Ireland. Sarge's "identification" consisted of opening up full blast and then trying to identify the aircraft.

Just let an airplane get close and Sarge would open up. He would then attempt to determine which side the plane was on.

FLOOR SHOW

Sarge taught Senior ROTC at St. Mary's of Texas in San Antonio. Each year they took their Seniors for two-weeks training at El Paso. Juarez was an exciting town.

At the time the soldiers were allowed to visit the main street only. Otherwise, too many were injured and robbed if they left the main street.

One of the instructors warned Sarge not to visit a certain night club. It seems that the instructor had visited this club and met an extremely attractive girl. As they became friendly she proposed a game. She said that she really liked him and would like to make love. But she liked to play games and he had to catch her first.

He went back to Fort Bliss and told his buddies about it. He said, "Talk about one athletic girl!" He said that he had a hell of a time catching her, over and under the furniture. But he did catch her and it was well worth it.

A few days later he and a buddy were in the bar and the same floor show came on. The lights went out, the ceiling was lit and sure enough there was another GI chasing the same girl.

All of his buddies wanted an autograph.

DOUG

While stationed at Londonderry, Northern Ireland, Sarge, Doug, Shockly and Kenny went downtown almost every night as long as they could beg, borrow or steal "6 and 6" (six shillings, six pence). With this amount they could buy one large bottle of English lite wine — just enough for the evening.

They met some nice Irish lasses and became friends. Doug liked Annie and they danced a lot. She invited ole Doug to a picnic in the forest. Doug read the wrong signals and tried to get a little on the side. Annie was incensed and told the group how mad she was. She said that if she had a knife she certainly would stick it in ole Doug.

Sarge took out his large fighting knife, opened it, and handed it to her. It was really comical. Ole Doug turned white and was frantically looking for a way out of there.

Later Doug was shot out of the war and sent home.

BAIT

Our unit had traveled across Africa from Port Say, Morocco to Tunisia to fight with the Africa Corps. We moved up one night and dug in near Hadjeb el Aioun, Tunisia. When we awoke in the morning, there was the whole German 18th Panzers, bumper to bumper, fueling. Three scout vehicles came up the road and we got two of them. One limped back up the road. The order came down to haul ass (retreat) at 1750 hours (5:30 p.m.). The Germans subjected us to our first unfriendly artillery fire.

We had made new camouflage nets in Port Say. The drivers thought they were being clever when they threw cactus on the nets for effect. When we took off they could not get the cactus off the nets and the Germans got some nice nets. Their infantry started a fire and movement action toward us. At 1750 we hit the road. As it got dark we passed through a whole British Armored Unit sitting track-to-track across the entire valley. They asked how we did. After we told them, they said, "Good show, Ole Mates." We realized why they were there. We were bait to draw the German heavy armor to them, to be slaughtered.

You may have used bait to catch fish and other things — but have you ever been bait?

Citizens of Port Say, Morocco are tying strips of cloth on netting for camouflage. The Germans took them away from us at our first meeting. Hadjeb el Aioun, Tunisia

The 37mm anti-tank gun that we used when we first
met the enemy proved to be too light for the job.

NAN

Nan, an Irish girl, was not too pretty but she was quiet and nice. She
plainly stated, "There would be no TLC."

This was the case in Ireland. If you wanted a little TLC you had
better show the girl a ring. Two of our guys got married in Ireland.

Sarge and Nan hit it off well to the delight of her father. Sarge would
sit in the honor seat at the fireplace and read comic books to Nan. Her
father would pat Sarge on the knee and tell his cronies that Sarge made
15 pounds ($60) per month, which was a lot of money in Ireland. Things
were going well. Sarge had a friendly place to relax after duty.

Unfortunately, Max hit a crap game and we took Nan's father out to
the pubs and he got really drunk. Later he went home and punched out
his wife. There went my girl chum and a trip to Dublin. He was my size
and had two suits. I was to go along as his son. Nan's attitude about sex
was kind of fortunate in a way. I got to eat most of my candy bars.

GIRL

We went into reserve at Benvento, Italy. Jessie must have met her there as that was the only time we were in the vicinity. This very charming girl latched on to our Jessie and proceeded to trail him all over Italy. It was unbelievable. We would move out in the middle of the night, travel many miles, dig in, sack out and there she would be. She would come into our position and crawl in with Jessie. In the morning the Ole Man would make Jessie send her down the road. Damned if she didn't show

up the next time we stopped. When we went into rest he would come through the outfit in search of a clean shirt. If he found one, he would head down the road to Benvento. He claimed her butler would meet him and clean his clothing. This went on for months. Suddenly he didn't need a clean shirt and he didn't go down the road anymore. This is still a mystery, even to his best friends.

Our Italian family had it rough.
We helped them all we could.
February 19, 1945.

MAX

Back in Casino, Sarge was on guard looking out the front door and Max was guarding his back. Out of three massive thick walls between the Germans and us there was only one wall left. Bullets would hit the last wall directly. Old Busy Bee fired a few bursts. At the same time we noticed what we thought were muzzle blasts flashing to our rear. The bullets hit the opposite side of the wall and ole Max, who was standing, slowly started sliding down the wall. Sarge thought that he was hit and called softly, "Max, Max are you hit?" He continued to slide. Sarge said again, "Max, Max are you hit?"

Finally he slid down all the way until he sat on the ground. He gave himself a good going over, turned his head slowly and said, "No."

That boy scares the crap out of me.

UNDERWEAR

We were in a defensive position west of the Fonduke Pass. There were little or no rations, so Sarge cleared it with the Lieutenant that he and a driver would attempt to get through the MP cordon and find a village and perhaps buy some food. (The Army set up MP lines so that soldiers could not butt out.)

We made it to a crowded village. It seems they were having a market day but they didn't have anything to sell. They would not trade for Limey cigarettes. Nothing was available, except for a poor skinny bird that an Arab claimed was a chicken. He said that he'd trade it for a pair of the Lieutenant's drawers that were in a muzet bag strapped on to the Jeep.

Back on the line we boiled the hell out of this miserable bird. The Lieutenant enjoyed gnawing on the little leg he got. Sarge clued him in on the cost of the chicken and he no longer had a change of drawers. Guess he really liked ole Sarge's cooking as he didn't react unfavorably.

STRANGE CUSTOMS

Maria lived with her family in a small, two room apartment in Napoli. As the sole provider, she entertained military boys in the only bedroom. The family all slept on the floor in the kitchen. One night she slipped from the bed of her benefactor and ran to the pot in its usual place in the corner of the bedroom. She proceeded to blow out all the romance of the evening. Strange customs in these foreign lands.

TITTY

The national dress for women in Korea, as Sarge sees it, is a long dress that begins high under the breasts and hangs to the ankles. A short jacket or shirt is worn over the shoulders.

While working around the mamasans at our school in Yugli-li, it was noticed that sometimes a titty peeked out from under the upper garment.

One day it was freezing cold. GIs were in arctic gear and zipped up to their noses. The women didn't seem to mind the cold on their bare skin. One would think that their nipples would freeze. Apparently they had been living in these conditions all of their lives and they were tough.

I don't remember if any of our guys offered them a hand.

BUMPS-A-DAISY

On our way to Africa, we traveled from Lurgin, Ireland, Strand Rae, Scotland to just north of Liverpool to a staging area in a huge mansion. People in Moberly were very good to us and invited us to their community center for dancing. They taught us the "Bumps-A-Daisy" — a dance designed to get us in shape to meet any enemy.

Sarge's partner was a stout lady about forty years old, who was cheerful and eager to maul him. The dance goes: one, two, and bump — the ole girl certainly knew how to bump. She bumped young Sarge halfway to Ireland, much to the hilarity of the other ladies. They did all they could to send us on our way with cheerful hearts.

We departed England for Africa from Liverpool on Christmas Day, 1942. Much to our delight we had turkey and all the trimmings on board the ship. The British ship, The Empress of Australia, had been taken from the Germans as reparations after WWI. She had been built so the Kaiser could travel in comfort to see the world that he had captured.

The ladies taught us not to show any lights even though we were way out in the country. If a German bombardier didn't drop his complete load of bombs, he would look for lights and if he spotted one, he would release the rest of his bombs.

Moberly, England, home of the energetic dancers. December, 1942.

AIRPLANES

Young Sarge and three other guys who were manning the position in Casino were lying around bullshitting, waiting for the war to end when the American Air Force showed up. We could not complain about air support but we did wish they were a little more accurate. One guy flew around looking and then went into his dive. Max yelled that he was going to hit us and damned if he didn't put his bomb right outside our house. We had already retreated into our four-man hole and were relatively safe until a piece of masonry as big as a basketball came crashing through our escape hole. One guy was able to divert it so that no one was injured. We agreed that what they were saying was true. When a British plane comes over, the Germans hit their holes. When a German plane comes over, the British hit their holes. When an American plane comes over, EVERYONE HITS THEIR HOLES!

If you complain, they say, "You're getting close cover, aren't you?"

CASSINO

LOOKING TO REAR FROM OUR
POSITION IN TOWN.

We had a four-man hole under here where we
would retreat when airplanes and artillery came in.

VISIT

Because of our mission in Europe (which was to block the Russians and Czechs should they come over the border), it wasn't easy for Infantry Company Commanders to be away from their commands. The situation was quiet so the Battle Group Commander gave Cap permission to go on leave. Cap wanted to show his wife, Doretta, many of the places he had been and talked about during WWII. They started at Pompeii, south of Naples, and followed the flow of the American advance up to Northern Italy. Along the way they visited the site near the Ripido River where her brother, Sidney, had been KIA. They visited Naples and Cap showed her that even in these modern days people live in caves. At Casino they found and visited with the family that Young Sarge and his platoon had befriended during the battle. The family lived in a new building. In fact, almost all of the buildings in Casino were new since they had been nearly wiped out by our war games. One of the girls lived in Rome so we went there to visit her. Typically male Italian, her husband was aloof and not too friendly until he read the introduction written on the back of a picture taken of his wife many years ago during the war. Then the wine flowed freely. He insisted that if we came back during the Olympic Games we could stay with him and keep our car in his garage. Rome was bursting with visitors at the time. This was a nice offer. Sarge and his guys had been good to her family when they were destitute during the war.

YOUNG ITALIAN

We were way north of Rome, in the attack, and were doing quite well. We stopped for a breather, set up our defense and started to regroup. We set up our guns around a farm complex. Ole Max and Sarge made themselves right at home and climbed into this clean and inviting bed, boots and all. We thought the villagers had all headed for the hills so we were surprised when a young Italian walked into the bedroom. We could see that he was not pleased that we were sharing his mother's bed. We could see that he wasn't too bright either because he started giving some lip to two armed men. Max eyeballed him for a minute or so. He'd had it with him, put a shell in the chamber of his carbine, pointed at the teener's stomach and said, "Pototomi vino." This was supposed to mean, "Bring me wine." There was a complete change in his attitude for the better.

I don't know where he got the wine because we had made a thorough search the night before. But he came in with a large demijohn of Dago Red. A chunk of bread would have been appreciated.

SHARING

Even when she was as poor as a church mouse, Sarge's mother taught him to share whatever he possessed. Throughout his career in the service if it were available, he carried a container of the national spirits. He would stop along the road and serve soldiers who were marching along. He did this in Korea whenever he had a reason to travel.

Some years later, he was visiting relatives in Iowa. His first cousin, Caroline, introduced him to her husband. They both eyeballed each other and thought that they had seen each other before. It seems that ole Lieutenant had served Ralphie a tall welcome drink on a lonely road on the DMZ in Korea. Guess the small world stuff applies here.

HANK

We had just won the battle of Hill 609 and were heading for Tunis, Tunisia. We were sailing across a wide barren mesa in broad daylight. We were unaccustomed to this as the Germans rarely let us move in the daylight. Hank was worried and was muttering to himself — things like, "They are near. They are going to shell us." Sarge was nervous so he told Hank to knock it off.

The Germans were all on boats heading for Italy. About that time an 88 came screeching in. In a flick of an eyelash ole Hank, in the ditch, looked over at Sarge in his ditch and said, "I told you so." We have a dilemma. Here we were out in the open and a German had a cannon to play with. The solution was to continue down this good road, go over a hill and dash into a small canyon. We were told that we would be in range when we came around the bend as the German was acting as if he were in a shooting gallery — and we were the targets. Under no conditions were we to stop on this road.

So away we went. Ole Hank was over the steering wheel of our Jeep like a seasoned Indy race car driver roaring around the corner. We came along and there sat Jessie in his Jeep with the road blocked. We headed for the little valley the best we could. Jessie turned around and we turned off right in front of him. He turned up a bank, turned his Jeep over, fell out of it and Hank almost hit him. To show the caliber of our guys — when we finally arrived into the small safe valley, we immediately took up the perpetual poker game that we had been playing on Hill 609. Hank still wouldn't believe Sarge when he said that there was no danger near.

Hank just loved this 88mm. He jawed at Sarge, when Sarge assured him that there was no one in the vicinity.

Hank and Sarge doing laundry in Bizerte. Note the truck hidden in the trees, safe from German airplanes.

STARKEY

He came to us as a replacement shortly before we attacked Casino. He was a wise guy who informed us that he was from "Philly" (Philadelphia, PA). He hadn't been indoctrinated to the rules of the game.

The night we pulled out of Casino, believe me, not one tear was shed over leaving our home. We assembled in a steep wadi (dry stream bed), rested the men and prepared for a long night of driving back from the front lines. We had to drive until a mountain would shield our headlights from the enemy. Blackout driving is slow, tedious and can be dangerous. We were particularly concerned that our drivers get some rest, so Sarge announced that the drivers were not to be disturbed. Ole Starkey just did not listen right. He kept bothering the squad driver. Max told him to

cut it out and Starkey challenged Max. As Platoon Sergeant, I told Max, "It's OK to give him a little on-the-spot training." So Max handed his rifle to Sarge, then his field glasses and his harness that carried a first aid packet, canteen, etc. Starkey jumped down from the truck. Max turned and hit ole Starkey right on the button. Starkey went down like a ton of crap. He finally made it to his feet and climbed into the truck. Old Philly came to be a great soldier that night.

Starkey (back row left) learned a good lesson at Casino.

CHICKEN

This true story didn't happen in any of the units in which Sarge served. It happened to a good buddy, a comrade in the VFW. He served fifty missions over Europe and is alive to tell about it.

Many times in the British Isles the airfields were placed on farms where there was enough distance for the airplanes to take off and land. There were usually many farm animals around the equipment.

Ed tells of the time that they took off for a mission. Lo and behold, there was a chicken perched right in the middle of the bomb rack. He gingerly retrieved the chicken and took it back to his seat. The chicken snuggled up and was apparently satisfied, except the chicken didn't have oxygen equipment and started to droop. Ed couldn't tolerate this so he put the chicken's head in his oxygen supply and the chicken perked up. During the rest of the mission Ed periodically revived the chicken so the chicken made it home.

At a ceremony for the crew the chicken was awarded an air mission medal. Ed always chuckles when he tells this story.

Market place in Fonduke Pass, in Africa, where Sarge made a big bargain for a chicken — at least, we thought it was a chicken.

BUGLER

Slim was our First Sergeant. He was a big, long gangly guy so it took some effort to dig a slit trench long and deep enough to get his butt below ground level. We moved up in Tunisia. Despite the First Soldier's duties he managed to dig a shallow trench. Things seemed to be going well when the Germans decided to harass us. They threw in a few shells and Slim headed for his hole. Just as he reached it the bugler jumped in first. Slim jumped on top of him. I can still hear Slim blessing the bugler while his big butt was standing out above ground level. Later the bugler was our first KIA.

First Sgt. Nelson (right) dug a big hole to get his butt below ground. The bugler helped him occupy it.

BLIND

The outfit was being relieved and they assembled in a large forest near the company trains (supply and cook shack). One platoon had been fortunate to find barrels of wine at their position. This called for a little alcohol production. It wasn't a problem to construct a still from wrecked truck parts. The still was made leakproof with invasion cement, which was placed on the engine and wiring before one came off the landing craft into deep water. Sarge got some sort of drink from the cooks and proceeded to have a party. He wasn't alone. The convoy started and they ground along until they came around a mountain and the MPs said to put on the headlights. There was great cheering from the guys who had been under blackout restrictions for months. Sarge cheered and then fell asleep. When he awoke he couldn't see the lights. He remembered the effects of wood alcohol blindness. He shouted to his driver, "Mike, I'm blind! I'm blind!" Before he went to sleep Sarge had inadvertently thrown a parka over his head. Mike helped him to see again by pulling the parka off Sarge's head. Mike said something about those so-and-so drunks. Sarge swore to never drink again. Wonder if he meant it?

HOLE

The mission of the 24th Division was to protect against the Russians and Czechs. We kept our soldiers in shape by maneuvers and marching across Bavaria. Cap, as Headquarters CO, was in charge of establishing Regimental Headquarters wherever the Colonel said we would stop for the night. Cap did not like the Regimental Executive Officer and thwarted him whenever he could get away with it.

There was a very large hole in the bivouac area for the night. The Exec told Cap that he wanted engineer tape around the hole. (This tape is similar to the yellow tape that U.S. law enforcement uses.)

Cap didn't tell the first soldier to do this because he hoped the Exec would fall into the hole. Our unit was entertaining some Forestmeisters this evening and knowing them, you know we imbibed more than a few. Someone outside called to Cap. As Cap charged out of the tent he fell into the deep hole. A he crawled up the steep banks of the hole, he was shouting, "First Sergeant, put some tape around this hole. Somebody's going to get killed out here!" Cap had snookered himself.

WATER

It was difficult to remain clean in the Tunisian desert. The one time we found water, we stripped, washed the only clothing that we had and we sat around in the sun and burned our hind-ends off. There are no shade trees in the desert.

The engineer shower units couldn't find water so we went without showers. When we reached Tunis we established our own shower. We wrecked out some large timbers from destroyed buildings, buried them and constructed a sturdy stand. We mounted two 55 gallon drums on the stands. Someone came up with a shower head and we were in business.

We filled the drums and waited a couple of days for them to heat up from the sun. That day while the outfit was out clearing German supply dumps, Sarge figured that he would take his shower while there was still plenty of hot water.

"Hot water!"

Sarge pulled the chain and damn near scalded himself. He never thought the African sun would make the water this hot.

All showers were taken in the morning, after a cool desert night.

TYPHUS IN NAPLES

When we were in Italy there was a typhus epidemic. We found their treatment of the populace rather entertaining. They set up teams of white coated persons on the street corner and would grab everyone and delouse them. To kill fleas, they would grab a person, stick a hose anywhere in their clothing and give them a tremendous dose of a white powder. We liked to watch the very proper, well dressed, old girls strolling the street only to be disgraced on the corner. It was fun to watch their faces as the powder squirted out from every opening in their clothing.

We helped by laughing uproariously. If looks could kill, all of the Yankees would be dead.

ARCHIE

Sarge was visiting Max's position one evening — just doing nothing, wondering if they were going to retire here on the Anzio Beachhead. A soldier walked through the door and Sarge looked at him and said, "Hi Arch." Archie said, "Hi Sarge."

Archie was Sarge's hero when he visited the town in which he was born. Sarge lived in Sioux City, Iowa but always went back to his grandpa's farm each summer as he was a little guy and could make their ball teams. Arch was catcher on the baseball team, fullback on the football team — an all around good guy in this little town. He always paid attention to the little kids.

He was on a recon mission to bring his unit through the next morning, when it was scheduled to break out of the Anzio perimeter. Arch needed a place to sleep that night. We fed him the best food that we had and arranged for a place to sleep. We dug through the cement floor of the living room and built a heavy roof over the hole.

Any shell that would reach us, would have to go through the roof, the upper floor and then our homemade roof. There was room for three guys to sleep comfortably; we had four, so we agreed that each man could choose his corner, climb in and crap out.

The following morning we gave Arch something to eat and he took off on his mission. Many years later, I found out that I was the last one to see Arch alive. He was KIA the day that he left us.

RATS

GIs and rats seem to go together like peanut butter and jelly.

Wherever you go, a bunker on the DMZ in Korea or a dilapidated building in Europe, the ole rat buddy would show up.

In 1942 we were quartered at a castle near the southern border of Ireland. The buildings were in an enormous rock quadrangle that resembled a fort. All animals, maintenance, vehicle storage, etc. were stored there. The EM were bunked in enormous hay mows. Sergeants were assigned to the tack room. Senior Sergeants lived in the caretakers cabin. Officers lived in the castle but were not allowed in the main house. They were happy in the maids quarters (although the maids had long since left). Rats were everywhere — in the walls at night, running across the floor. If PX rations finally found us, 11 chewable products had to be kept in tin cans or the rats would have a feast. Candy bars were always, in most countries, used for a little honey loving. Sarge ate all of his candy bars because he figured there would always be a little honey available down the road. But candy bars were hard to come by.

The Old Man was so concerned about his troopies that he asked the medics to help us to eradicate the rats. A spit and polish Medical Officer showed up and told us, "Yes, rats do eat. The more they have to eat the more of them there will be. The less they have to eat the less there will be of them." It was fortunate that he departed because our First Soldier stood up and said, "Men, all together, one, two, three — bullshit!" That pretty much summed up our opinion of how to remove a rat infestation.

Training on 37mm gun in the courtyard of our
rat-infested quarters in Ireland.

HONEY BUCKETS

During WWII the British were forced to establish camp and quarter all over Great Britain. They erected thousands of quonset huts and stuffed troops into the many manor houses left over from their days of exploitation around the world. Most of the mansions were vacant and unoccupied. To handle those who went potty every day they built long open sheds with a number of potty holes. Under each hole was a honey bucket. The most detested duty was the daily honey bucket brigade. This brigade caused most soldiers to behave so they could miss their turn. This night soil was collected by farmers and sprayed onto the fields by the honey wagon.

Now you know why Irish potatoes are so delicious.

In Germany we always knew when it was spring as our nostrils could detect the odor of the honey wagons. It was not too long ago that the great Northwest discontinued this type of fertilizer.

Isn't this topic informative?

TRENCH FOOT

On the Winter Line in the mountains in Italy, in 1944, it was not unusual to see a soldier coming down the trail or road with his boots in his hand — completely oblivious that he was walking barefoot through ice and icy water. His feet were for all intents and purposes, dead. He had trench foot. This was caused by not removing his boots for many days, perhaps weeks.

Soldiers did not remove foot gear while sleeping as enemy fire of many kinds might cause them to seek shelter. They needed their boots on so that they could "cut a choggie" (a Korean expression that means "to get the hell out of there!").

A wound that will take you all the way back to the United States and out of danger is called a "million dollar wound." Trench foot was not considered a million dollar wound but most of these boys lost their feet.

SOCKS

During WWII our President's lady, Eleanor Roosevelt, came into considerable disfavor when she insisted that our soldiers be issued sufficient socks. This was another expense for the government. Our economists did not plan for this expense in the war budget estimate. However, she saved millions of feet.

Soldiers in combat must be ready to move out immediately; thus, they do not remove their shoes for days, sometimes weeks. Their feet can deteriorate or rot. The troopies called this condition, "trench foot."

To help keep our guys on the line, they were issued three pairs of socks. They were required to wear one pair in the helmet, one pair was fastened inside their shirt on the left side for which a large safety pin was provided. The reason for the left side is that a leader keeps his squad, platoon, etc., records in a notebook over his heart, which is known as the live file. This way if a leader is put out of action the next in command will know where the records are. This was an easy method that all could learn. A soldier did not have the option when to change his socks. Whenever the action slowed down, his sergeant and officer would set him down on his poncho and visually inspect his feet. If they looked suspicious, the medic would begin treatment immediately.

Our guys loved and heartily thanked Eleanor. She kept a lot of our guys on the line and saved their feet.

WOUNDED GERMAN

Before we could move on to our objective — Chicina, Italy — our guys had to take a Fascist complex on the edge of town. When Sarge arrived on the scene with his platoon, he saw a poignant sight.

A very young German, no more than a boy, was lying on the ground severely wounded. A gigantic, bearded American walked over to the boy and tenderly lifted him from the ground. He nodded to his Jeep driver to pull up behind him. When the Jeep arrived the Sergeant stepped back onto the bumper and climbed up until he was sitting on the Jeep hood. He signaled forward with his head and off they went to the aid station. Some youngster probably went home to his mother at the end of hostilities.

BED SPRINGS

One time on the Anzio Beach, one of Sarge's troopies told him that he had detected some movement across the line. This being highly unusual, Sarge had to take a look. Sarge and a few other observers were looking through the cracks that had been sawed through the shutters. We saw movement all along the front, which called for artillery fire. We were extremely accurate as every position had an identical map. All Sarge had to do was shoot the direction and distance from his position and give the sight setting to the gunner.

A funny thing happened. Just as the artillery communication man said, "On the way," a German with his coat flapping, dashed from behind a hedge. When the barrage hit the ground, he jumped into a large hole. As the barrage hit he came straight up from the hole and took off and disappeared behind the hedge. This was so incongruous that all of the observers had a hearty laugh.

We all agreed that it looked as if the hole were full of bed springs and he did a trampoline maneuver. We also agreed that he probably had to change his drawers after the way we had entertained him.

TRANQUILITY

Every infantryman is issued a half of a tent, called a "shelter half," which includes a tent pole and about six stakes. Two soldiers combine this equipment to make a "pup tent" for some shelter from the elements.

If you have been in this business long enough, you can manage to acquire both halves and then create your own little "mansion." Believe it or not, there is much pleasure to be had out on the desert when you're in the reserve and no one is shooting at you.

Sarge pitched his tent on a hillside in the desert, spread out his blanket on the sand, used his helmet as a pillow, lit a little piece of candle, reclined and thoroughly enjoyed his evening while reading at home. His surroundings were tranquil and he enjoyed the cool desert breeze. His stomach was full of "C" ration and sufficient water. What could be better?

The only hitch was that a candle in a pup tent causes the tent to glow, which can be seen by aircraft for miles. After much combat you can hear an aircraft at greater distances. So when you hear that faint drone you must snuff out the candle immediately and lie quietly until the aircraft goes away. Then you can resume your tranquil evening.

Most people cannot believe that the tent can be a very homey abode. But you can learn to appreciate the small things.

CHEEKS

After the African Campaign in the spring of 1943 our unit moved back to Oran, Algeria. To maintain our skills we frequently trained out in the desert. We were doing a location problem by studying a map laid out on the hood of a Jeep. A young, inquisitive Arab saw us gathered around the Jeep and chose to join us. He kept getting closer and closer. As no one challenged him he joined our circle around the Jeep.

We were all very focused on studying the map. The young Arab was (unfortunately) standing between Max and Sarge. Max nodded at Sarge, who reached down and squeezed one of the Arab's cheeks. Max squeezed the other one. If you've ever seen an Arab in a hurry, you should have seen this guy. He dug out of there. The last we saw of him was his white robe floating behind him as he ran over the hill. I imagined that he talked about this incident to others in his village. He probably told them about the two horny Americans who hadn't had a female for months.

Private, Howitzer Company,
Sioux City, 1939

HOWARD

Back in 1939, Sarge, a Private First Class (PFC), was assigned to Howitzer Company, 133rd Infantry, Iowa National Guard in Sioux City. The unit went to Camp Dodge, Des Moines, for its annual two weeks of intensive training. Every Company had a boxing team.

Howard, whose total weight was eighty pounds, qualified as the featherweight contender. He was on the kitchen crew and every time the men went through the chow line they had to listen to a litany of how he was going to destroy all of his opponents. The great night came and the men escorted Howard to his corner. He leapt into the ring, furiously shadow boxing and knocking out his imaginary opponents. When he slowed down from his gyrations, he glanced into the opposite corner and saw his opponent. He stopped. He was stunned when he saw a muscular boy, a head taller and at least fifty pounds heavier with scary leopard swim trunks. From then on Howard never took his eyes off the guy. Howard went back to his corner and plunked down on the stool. When the referee called him to the center of the ring, Howard never moved. One guy shoved him. When he was off balance another guy grabbed the stool and Howard had to stand up. He trudged to the center of the ring, got his instructions, and surprisingly, he came out flailing like a windmill. There was much flailing and little landing until Howard backed out of the melee holding his crotch and shouting, "Foul, foul. He hit my nuts!"

After a conference in Howard's corner, Howard was disqualified for refusing to continue. He claimed that his nuts hurt.

Needless to say the men never heard fight talk in the chow line again. Until the day he died Howard claimed that the guy deliberately hit him in his gonads.

Howard and Sarge's squad in Camp Dodge, Des Moines, IA, 1939

Our little 37mm Howitzer was not an anti-tank gun. Were we were supposed to battle 88s with this little thing?

Private,
Anti-Tank
Company,
Sioux City, 1940

MY-O-MY

On the Anzio Beachhead in Italy there was a stalemate for over four months. The soldiers were completely surrounded by the Germans and Italians. This meant that for over four months they were never outside in the daylight. All activities were done under the cover of darkness.

Every structure, valley, road and grove of trees were named. This identification system provided a great savings in time when they wanted to call in artillery or report strange things going on across the line.

Across from the men, about 500 yards or so, was a beautiful stand of trees identified as Bellou Woods. One night they were informed that a time on target (TOT) was to be placed on Bellou Woods. This meant that they would shoot practically every weapon, even a Navy cruiser, in an attempt to completely destroy the enemy strong point at Bellou Woods.

You haven't lived until you've experienced this show of power. What an awesome display! It is true that a cruiser artillery round sounds like a box car flying through the atmosphere.

After the shot, the woods were no longer there. The soldiers assumed that no living thing could possibly survive this type of punishment. But to their amazement, the silence was broken by a German who could speak English. He crawled out of somewhere and called across the line, "My-o-my." He was like an angry mother castigating a naughty child.

SINGING GUNS

After the African Campaign the men returned to Oran, Algeria and began training, especially for their replacements. They went south of Oran down into the Sahara Desert. It seemed like a typical movie scene, including an authentic French Foreign Legion fort. An old timer came over from the fort to look at everything the men did. He seemed like a pest. The allies had set up an anti-tank range with actual moving targets and the men could shoot live ammunition.

When you fire a 57mm high velocity weapon you must make sure that you are behind the shield. The muzzle blast is terrific and it can knock you to the ground.

The old timer kept edging toward the muzzle of the gun so Sarge gave the order to fire. Amazingly, the old timer didn't seem too distressed.

The next morning Sarge had good reason to feel super crappy. The old Legionnaire presented Sarge with three bottles of wine to be served to the crew of the "Singing Gun."

ROLLING BARRAGE

If you ever have the opportunity to follow a rolling barrage, turn it down.

During the African Campaign an old tactic perfected in WWI was used to great effect against the Germans and Italians in Tunisia. In the attack, following the initial barrage, the rolling barrage is used to keep the enemy heads down while our guys advance.

Only an incredibly stupid person would raise his head up to fire while artillery is going off around him.

After the campaign, some brilliant staff officer suggested to the Commanding General that every troopie in the 34th Division should have the opportunity to follow a barrage. So they moved us down into the desert to an artillery training range. Even though this was a bad idea, we all had to go.

The game was for the artillery to fire a salvo over our heads. (A salvo is a discharge of a number of artillery pieces in a regular succession.) We were to advance a certain distance, fire another salvo and then advance. If all went well and there were no short rounds, you got to the top of the hill in one piece. It was our turn in the lion's mouth, so Ole Top lined us up either during or after a salvo, Sarge wasn't sure. He screamed, "Forrrrward!" and as the salvo exploded he screamed, "Haaaalt!"

Now this horse manure went on for an eternity.

Trying to minimize his chances of getting shrapnel in his heart or testicles, Sarge carried his rifle diagonally across his body in hopes that it would deflect shrapnel toward some other guy.

As they reached the top of the hill and the firing stopped, Sarge checked his heart and crotch and found both to be in excellent condition.

SICILY

After the African Campaign, the Company stayed near Tunis on a staging area assignment. Our mission was to support units who were making the Sicilian invasion. There were many large, barbed wire enclosures constructed out on the desert for housing prisoners expected to be captured during the invasion. We were all set to be prison guards when we looked up the road and here came our first customers from the port of Tunis. It was unbelievable. There were four men across for as far as we could see — a gray-blue line of Italian soldiers.

At the end of the Italian heroes were perhaps fifty or so Germans. The Italians were talking, laughing and joking as they were out of a war that they didn't want. The Germans were defiant, still full of fight even though they were in a sorry state.

The whole procession was followed by meat wagons (ambulances) of which the Italians were happy to jump aboard. The Germans refused to ride and were carrying and dragging their wounded. In the compounds we had to separate the Germans as they disrespected the Italians and would attack them. Some Italians had brought provisions with them. This was an indication that most of them had not planned to defend Sicily. It was understood that their good buddy Germans had treated them shabbily in the division of ammo and supplies.

Our guys didn't mind guarding the Italians because the Italians didn't want to get away.

BRAVE BOXERS

One evening Max, Doug, Kenny and Sarge were coming home from the nightly dance in Londonderry. There was a shortage of utilities caused by the war so the dances lasted only a few hours. After that the GIs were free to roam. As he walked by the auditorium in the twilight, Sarge could barely read the sign out front. It listed the weekly prize fights and participants that were needed. Never to miss a beat, Sarge could see some "3 and 6" money here. With three shillings, six pence he could buy a bottle of English light wine. They'd never touch the stuff at home but they weren't at home, so they drank whatever was at hand. Then and there, Sarge's fight stable was born.

As Sarge was prone to get into small incidences, he surrounded himself with big dumb guys, Doug and Kenny. The following morning, right after exercises, Sarge obtained two sets of boxing gloves from the supply room and proceeded to train his stable. While putting gloves on his pugilists he explained the science of self defense: the jab, right cross, left hook, uppercut, etc. Doug and Kenny eyeballed each other and attacked. There was such grunting, snorting, giggling, thump, thumps, "hee hees" . . . then more giggling and windmilling. At this disgusting sight, Sarge turned on his heels, walked back to his quarters, sat down, put his hands behind his head and pondered another source of 3 and 6.

57mm

Young Sarge had gone to the British 57mm anti-tank gun school in Sou karas, Algeria. Now that the African Campaign was over the men could do some serious training with the weapon. They went down to the Singing Guns Range where they could actually shoot the weapon.

The 57mm had a long barrel. In order to raise or lower it with the elevation wheels, the British put a heavy flash-hider on the end of the barrel. The dual purpose of the flash-hider was to break up the muzzle flash so that the enemy would have a difficult time finding the gun's location after it was fired. Evidently they ran out of flash-hiders so they substituted a cast iron collar around the end of the barrel.

On firing day Sarge yelled, "Fire one round." The soldiers fired one round then began taking casualties. A man next to Sarge grabbed his hip and fell to the ground. Another soldier, who had been reading while sitting in a truck, fell out of the truck. Sarge said, "Cease fire!"

It seems that the barrel had expanded and caused the cast iron barrel to become very hot shrapnel. So the search was on for flash-hiders.

Sarge had three of these 57mm (British 6-Pounders) in his platoon. They handled German armor much better than the little 37mm. Sarge was pulled off the line and sent to a British school in Algeria, where he learned all about them. He returned to his unit and taught others to use the weapon. He used British fire orders and nomenclature, causing confusion at first.

IRATE MESS SERGEANT

Our Company was in position, defending a portion of the front line in Tunisia in the spring of 1943. A mess sergeant came forward with his truck and crew to feed his unit the evening meal. He came to a small trail-like road behind our positions. Slim was guarding the road so the Sergeant asked him if the road had been mined. The Germans were prolific in their mining activities in Tunisia.

Slim told him that we had used the road all the time so it must be safe. As Sarge stopped to jaw with Slim there was an enormous explosion up the road. Suddenly Slim's eyes opened wide and he evacuated the area. A pissed off Sergeant came down the road with his rifle in hand. He was looking for the son-of-a-bitch who said the road had been cleared.

Sometimes retreat, or hide and seek, is indicated to stay healthy.

MESS TRUCK BACKS OVER MINES

We were on our approach to the last great battle for North Africa, Hill 609 (the number always designated the height of the hill). We hid out in a gully or small valley. We had been severely shelled earlier in the day. Sarge's brother-in-law was in another valley and had witnessed the shelling. He had stated that no one could have come out of our barrage alive. We did, however, because there was a steep little stream bed and we managed to get most of our guys down into it.

We took casualties but there were no KIAs. Our mess truck found us that evening and we had a rare, warm, complete meal. As the 3/4 ton truck backed up to leave, it ran over two teller anti-tank mines that the Germans had stacked for power. They got satisfaction. The mines blew the truck straight up into the air. It turned around and upside down.

It was mandatory that all of the vehicle floors were packed with sand bags to reduce the shrapnel effect of ripped out floor boards, or anything else that could be hurled. Fortunately, the mess crew was blown clear and survived. But the truck was totaled.

As the crew walked out they said some very unkind things about the soldiers who were walking around on top of the destruction and didn't even know it. But we all thanked the good ole sand bags.

EVERYBODY GOES TO CHURCH

When an army unit is not actively fighting, it is subject to many kinds of harassment — U.S. Savings Bonds, personal saving accounts, church attendance, and more.

During a briefing of Company Commanders of our 19th Infantry Battle Group in Augsburg, Germany, the Colonel stated that Chaplain had reported that attendance by church members of our BG was very low. So he made a strong statement about how he wanted his men to go to church. Later at their daily coffee klatch the Company Commanders agreed that in order to increase attendance there would be no passes issued on Sunday, and that there would be a mandatory formation in class "A" uniform — all spit and polish.

They marched 1700 soldiers to a church that at best held 150 persons. When the Colonel arrived for church he could not believe this perfect attendance record that was set. He dismissed the formation and the men went on their way. Sarge went to church but that's another story.

CHAPPIE

After the Company Commanders had marched their troops to church, they received many letters from U.S. Congressmen over this incident because many troopies never intended to attend church services.

Cap decided to surprise his ole buddy, the Chaplain. He called him "Chappie" and they were drinking buddies — although Cap could not keep up with the holy drinker.

The night before they had had a few drinks, in fact, quite a few. Chappie had a habit of giving everyone a comradely pat on the back, which just about floored the recipient. Captain told him that one more pat like that and he was going to deck ole Chappie on his hind end.

The organ sounded off and ole Chappie came in wearing a filmy white robe. He waltzed out and turned to bless the congregation. He flung out his arms, spotted Cap and forgot the lines that he had rehearsed for this performance. After he had tended his flock, he went to the rear door and said "Good-bye." As Cap and his wife reached the door, Chappie told Cap's wife, "He made me lose my mind."

They remained good friends and met many years later in the Far East. They did not toast each other with spirits because Chappie had seen the light. He was now Chief Chaplain of the South Pacific Theater.

MESS TENT

Sarge has always enjoyed teaching. As a Company Commander he taught his officers many pitfalls of command.

In Germany, Gene was a young Lieutenant, Executive Officer of Cap's Company. One day he learned a good lesson in diplomacy. Gene was HQ Company Mess Officer. He and Cap were having a meeting with the Battle Group Executive Officer regarding the set up of the Battle Group Headquarters — including the set up and security of the mess tent. This tent was designed by some bureaucrat who had never been in the field and probably didn't know his rear end from second base. The tent he designed had many elevations which required many lengths of tent poles.

Our troopies had enough trouble with their Tinker Toys™ let alone this mess of lengths to contend with. We preferred a squad tent, which had only two poles that easily went up and down even in the blackest of nights.

The Executive Officer liked the sight of the mess tent standing there in all its glory. He asked if we were bringing the mess tent and Cap replied that he was, amid glares from Gene. The EO asked Cap again if he was bringing the mess tent and Cap replied in the affirmative amid more glares from Gene.

As they left the meeting Cap looked at Gene and said, "Don't bring the mess tent." Gene looked confused so Cap told Gene that he had learned a valuable lesson on how to answer unreasonable requests.

When the Executive Officer saw the squad tent placed in perfect enfilade with perfect security, he had nothing to say. He had been snookered and accepted it.

LIVING QUARTERS

Shortly after arriving in Ireland, the outfit was stationed at a small Camp of Nissen huts, called Derrygally near Londonderry — a very crude and basic camp. Pure pine boards were laid across some sawhorses about six inches tall. To save material the mattresses were shaped like a body, broad at the top and tapering to a point where the legs were. It was impossible to remain on these mattresses while sleeping.

Coal space heaters were lined with concrete so little heat escaped into the room. The men broke the lining for more heat radiation. The British came around and charged the U.S. Government for every stove.

There was never enough coal so the soldiers went next door where the British had been stationed and liberated their coal. There was no hot water in the showers. Actually the men were well off but didn't know it because this was the last time in many months that even substandard showers were available.

After you and your buddies have lived without soap and water, you just don't realize that you stink to high heaven.

The British had supper ready. The men began to eat but they thought their throats had been cut. British rations were skimpy at best. They eat five times a day: breakfast, tea, lunch, tea, and dinner. With all these meals they really do not get very much to eat. There is a lot of tea served along with crackers, which are called "biscuits." Maybe this encourages people into thinking that they are getting something substantial.

The soldiers traveled through Lurgen on the way to Scotland and then down to Liverpool to go to Africa. It was getting late and they were hungry. The British Sergeant assured the men that the mess could service thousands of meals in a hurry. But the soldiers figured they could only serve that many in a hurry if the troops were not given any food. And they imagined that those miserable meals (only dabs of slop) were fairly expensive for the U.S.

For the first few weeks in the desert of Tunisia the soldiers were on British rations and they damn near starved to death.

SERGEANT OF THE GUARD

Shortly after arriving in Ireland, Sarge was assigned as Sergeant of the Guard. The Officer of the Guard was a fresh Lieutenant on his first tour of duty. We learned to love him but he was KIA in Africa.

One of our guys came through the main gate after dark. Lt. told Sarge to give him a prophylactic as he had been to Londonderry and was exposed to those "dirty, disease-ridden Irish girls." Little did he know that Irish girls didn't put out, period. If you wanted a little, you married her or nothing. Two of our guys married Irish girls but not because they were hard up. They loved the girls and brought them home.

This boy had never been near an Irish girl and was frightful of a pro. He hid under his bed, where Sarge found him. Sarge took him to the dispensary. Because he was too inebriated to treat himself it fell upon the Corpsman to do so. One part of the treatment was massaging cream onto the penis. The soldier loved this part of the treatment and giggled with pleasure. All the while the Corpsman was cussing out his patient as he was doing his duty. The Company Commander stopped this type of guard duty as being nonessential. "No love'n, no pros."

Rifle squad leader,
Camp Claiborne, LA, 1941.

82

A typical mess hall and orderly room
at Camp Claiborne, LA

ARTICLES OF WAR

The Articles of War are the Bible of the Army. It tells of all the crimes and omissions a soldier can do after his country has called him to cheerfully serve in her armed forces. At Camp Claiborne, LA evidently the Chaplain had something on the Regimental Commander or the Commander was zealous. Each Sunday regardless of race, color or creed, every soldier had to go to church.

Sarge had studied pre-history and animism so he knew that in no way was this religion stuff a valid belief. He refused to go to church so he was obliged to listen to The Articles of War. One can stand this torture for only so long. Then Sarge along with some other holdouts gave in and went to church. They didn't pray to this mythical God or Jesus something but they prayed mightily for their First Sergeant Slim.

RESPITE

The young soldier was hot, sweaty and very weary. He spied a fresh water pool in the mountains. As he entered the pond, he noticed a beautiful, brown-eyed maiden. Her eyes were luminous as she looked into his azure Irish eyes. They advanced toward each other, eyes locked and arms extended. As they got closer to each other, a "thump" was heard, followed by a "whup, whup" of tumbling mortar shell. The shell fell between them and ended the shortest courtship in history.

SERGEANT OF THE GUARD #2

A shot rang out in the night. Sarge figured that it came from the Nisson hut occupied by his own platoon. He heard the new Lt. coming so he put his boots up on the desk and feigned sleep. When the new Lt. arrived and informed him of the shot he said that he would handle it. He took off on a beeline to his hut. What a sight. Here was ole Max conducting a fist fight by holding a candle above the pugilists. It seemed that during the turmoil preceding the fight, one man accidentally discharged his rifle while cleaning it — an inexcusable mistake. Here was a hole in the ceiling to be explained. As it was his platoon, Sarge had to resort to some way out — some fiction to get his guys off the hook when he wrote the Guard Report. Everyone got off the hook except the shooter who paid mightily for his error.

INVIGORATING PRIVY

If you want to take a cruise to Europe over the North Sea during rough weather and ride the roller coaster at the same time, take a British troop ship. Many of these ships had been holiday vacation ships in peacetime. They did not have sufficient privies for all of the troopies. To solve this important dilemma they constructed privies over the side of the fantail (the rear of the ship). The privies jutted out from the hull so that when a person was seated, the only thing between his bare end and the roaring sea was air. It was said that even if you didn't have to go — you would. This reminds me of the saying, "It scared the crap out of me."

BOUNCING BETTY

"Betty" was not a vivacious Italian senorita but a very dangerous weapon of war. It was designed as an anti-personnel weapon. It was buried in the ground with three prongs sticking up. When the prongs were depressed, a canister of 350 ball bearings would jump six feet in the air and explode. A man had little chance of surviving.

At the Third Crossing of the Volturno River in Italy, Platoon Sergeant Carol was reconning an orchard when he stepped on a Bouncing Betty. He was KIA.

We were about a hundred miles north of Naples and the Crossing was protecting the German Gothic Defensive Line, anchored at Casino. After Carol's accident the CO called all NCOs to disarm a bomb. If the NCO refused, the NCO was demoted to Private on the spot. To disarm a bomb you had to find a pin and put it through a hole in the plunger. We all wondered how we could find the pin since the German soldier who armed the bomb probably played "hide the pin."

From then on when we ransacked a village we were on the alert for any item that might serve as a pin. Booby traps were all over the place. One guy went into a tall building, tripped a wire and brought the whole building down on him. He was KIA at the Third Crossing.

Later we ran into shoe mines, dainty little mines made of wood so that our minesweepers couldn't detect them. They would blow off at least a foot.

During our stay in the area Sarge hoped that none of his guys would find a Betty. He'd have to disarm it and the thought made him nervous.

SUPPLY DUMP

When the soldiers took Bizerte from the Germans they didn't have time to destroy everything so they left many supply dumps. Sarge's unit was to clean up a large dump. They issued food and supplies to other units. They served much of the food to their own guys and hauled the large artillery shells to a central dump. What remained was an enormous mound of just about every type of ammunition and flares that one could imagine. Sarge and his guys figured that the best way to clean this up was to destroy it. There were large bundles of cordite, which was used in the great coast artillery guns behind the rounds to give propulsion and send the rounds on their way to a target.

Sarge broke down the bundles of cordite and overlapped them into to a deep drainage ditch on the edge of about a square, city-block-size field. One guy lit the cordite and hit the ditch. Talk about a war zone! The whole area went to hell. Artillery shells exploded, belts of machine gun rounds went off and flares went every which way.

One Arab on a bicycle sped up to avoid being shot in the hind end. All in all, it was one damn fine explosion! People heard about it from many sources. But the men couldn't take it back and, fortunately, no one got killed. Still they did a fine job of cleaning up the place in a hurry.

AT THE MOVIES

One night while the GIs were in Bizerte, Tunis, they watched films on an outdoor screen some distance from town. They were engrossed in a plot when a much more exciting scenario was played out over the port. The Germans were pulling a spectacular air raid and the soldiers became cheering spectators. The cheering soon turned to groans as they realized: *What goes up must come down!*

Tons of used anti-aircraft shells and bullets began to pelt the men. There was no cover available so Sarge (who was slim) tried to crawl underneath a heavy soldier, who was unappreciative that he could protect a Sergeant.

Some of the Navy rockets were a yard long. One lit right next to Sarge's brother-in-law. These could cut a man in half if they hit him.

AIR RAID AT BIZERTE

There was a spectacular castle on the shore of the Mediterranean Sea, near the bivouac area. The Axis had used it as an observation post until the GIs took it from them. An air raid siren went off in nearby Bizerte.

Sarge and his friends decided to go to the castle to get a clear view of the raid. It was a bright, moonlit night. What they didn't realize was that their Jeep would be a dark target on a silvery road. But they thought that they could beat the game by speeding down the road.

The plane dropped a bomb. If it hadn't been for a bend in the road that bomb may have landed near them. Instead the bomb hit and knocked down a gigantic tree to their right.

The driver immediately turned left and went to a fortification on the hill. The men bailed out and went to an ammunition room deep in the fortification. They were content to rest there and reflect on what a stupid decision they had made, especially since they had survived the African Campaign and the many attempts the Germans had made to kill them.

BORDELLO #3

One night in a little Arab village in Algeria, North Africa, Max, Little Billy, Kenny and Sarge went out for a little excitement. They had just enjoyed an elevating experience on the front lines in Tunisia and needed a little harmless entertainment. Lo and behold they found another bordello. They were a little suspicious as the occupants were friendly.

Max wasn't feeling well because a few days before he had hit his head on some cobblestones. Sarge was broke again and could not afford the merchandise. By now he had swapped off the little loot he had.

As they reclined in the parlor and waited for the other guys, Max motioned Sarge toward the darkened bar. Sarge crept into the bar and shopped up some bottles of some kind of fluid. They had on their large tanker jackets so Max and Sarge could conceal three bottles each under their jackets.

Suddenly the MPs arrived. Max and Sarge bolted out of what they considered the back way. They handed their bottles over the wall and then pulled Billy over. They sat straddling the wall, defying the MPs, inviting them to move closer. No way were the MPs going to get any closer as these guys were still in combat gear and they looked rough.

Billy claimed that he had been gypped because as soon as the MPs came in his girl took off. Sarge demanded that Billy get a full refund.

The Madam said that she didn't see Billy. So Max and Sarge reached behind the wall and put ole Billy on display. He resented this and demanded that he be dropped, which he was.

The MPs said to shove off. These MPs from Iowa were uncouth. They could not recognize good Vermouth so they destroyed all six of the bottles.

This was their last bordello experience in Africa — or anywhere else for that matter. They dropped into a dry stream bed and sauntered off to new adventures.

44 CALIBER REVOLVERS

The soldiers had just taken a Fascist headquarters in a beautiful mansion just north of Rome. Sarge's platoon bedded down in the mansion for a good night's sleep. Sarge had warned his men about possible booby traps. But the building had been occupied by the enemy up until the time the soldiers moved in so they doubted that it was booby trapped.

Sarge got up first and there were his guys sleeping all over the beautiful parlor. Some of the divans looked like velvet.

Sarge headed for where he thought the orderly room would be. Here he found a wall of small compartments with doors that pulled up from the bottom and just dropped closed. He was in a hurry as the guys might awaken. He pulled up one door, dropped it and stopped in disbelief. There were two beautiful 44 caliber revolvers, still with their ordinance repair tags on them. They did not have trigger guards. Triggers were fitted underneath and dropped when the hammer was pulled back.

The Commanding General had ruled that when a soldier captured loot, it would be his after he left the Division. Meanwhile, it was to be turned in to the Supply Sergeant for safekeeping.

These guns were valuable and Sarge really wanted to get them home. He received the ultimatum to leave ordinance in Europe or be shipped back over if caught taking them home. So he opted to sell them in Italy. He sold them to a Liberty Ship Captain for $25 and a carton of cigarettes.

Doretta — the girl that
Sarge left behind in 1941.

Doretta had doubled
the family when
Sarge was stationed
in Derrygally, North
Ireland. Denny had
to wait two and a
half years to meet
his Daddy.

ABOUT THE AUTHOR

Herbert M. Youngdahl was born in Lake City, Iowa on September 2, 1921 to Eva and Verner Youngdahl. Most of his years through high school were spent in Sioux City, Iowa. In February 1939 he joined the Howitzer Company, 133rd Infantry, 34th Division in Sioux City. On February 10, 1941 the Company, was designated Anti-Tank and called to active duty. The Division was sent to Camp Claiborne, LA. In December 1941 the unit was sent to Europe. Arriving in Belfast, Northern Ireland, on January 15, 1942, they were the first Expeditionary Force to arrive in Europe in WWII. Of the millions of troops sent that way, Youngdahl estimates that he was about the one-thousandth person to go down the gangplank. The Division trained and was part of the island's defense until December 1942. Youngdahl was promoted from Rifle Squad Leader to Platoon Sergeant. On Christmas Day, 1942, the Division sailed from Liverpool, England to Oran, North Africa.

After occupying defensive positions along the Mediterranean Sea in Morocco, the Division moved eastward to contact the Germans and Italians in Tunisia. Here the Division was mauled badly by Rommel but lived to drive the Axis out of Africa. The 34th ran staging areas for Sicilian Campaign and received replacements and equipment lost in the Tunisian Campaign. In September the 34th followed the 36th (Texas) Division onto Blue Beach, south of Naples, Italy. The 34th kept pressure on Axis, traveling the length of the boot of Italy and wound up in Austria.

In Africa, Youngdahl participated in battles at Fonduk Pass, Kasserine Pass, and Hill 609. At Hill 609 he almost lost an arm because of an infected wound — but he was given a new drug called Sulfanilamide, which helped to save it.

The most pleasurable Battle was the Battle of the Casbah in Oran — with wine, women, and song.

In Italy, Youngdahl participated in battles of the Vulturno River Crossings, San Pietro, Casino, and the Anzio Beachhead. During the breakout at Anzio, he wound up in a MASH hospital with a concussion.

The following morning a doctor patted Youngdahl's stomach and asked, "How's your tummy, Soldier? What can I do for you?"

Youngdahl said, "A shot of whiskey would do just fine."

Soon a nurse came in with a shot of real American whiskey.

After Youngdahl downed the whiskey she handed him orders back to his outfit on the line. This was his shortest "R&R" ever.

The 34th set the record for days in combat in WWII. They had over 500 days on their Morning Report.

Youngdahl was a Tech Sergeant, Chief of Section at Headquarters 4th Army, Fort Sam Houston, San Antonio, Texas. His combat experience led to his promotion to Second Lieutenant Infantry. What a let down — going from a powerful Non Commissioned Officer (NCO) to a "shavetail" in one day.

From 1953 to 1954 Youngdahl served in Korea with the 2nd Infantry Division. He retired as a Captain Company Commander, Headquarters Company, 1st of the 19th Infantry, 24th Division, Augsburg, Germany on September 1, 1961.

Youngdahl has always enjoyed telling stories about his most humorous experiences. Many of his friends have suggested that he write about them. He thought they had a great idea and his writing evolved into this book.